The Graham Mansion

Also By Thomas D. Perry

Ascent To Glory: The Genealogy of J. E. B. Stuart

The Free State of Patrick: Patrick County Virginia In The Civil War

Images of America: Patrick County Virginia

Images of America: Henry County Virginia

Then and Now: Patrick County Virginia

Notes From The Free State Of Patrick:
Patrick County, Virginia, and Regional History

God's Will Be Done: The Christian Life of J. E. B. Stuart

Patrick County Oral History Project: A Guide

J. E. B. Stuart's Birthplace: A Guide for Educators and Visitors

Upward Toil: The Lester Family of Henry County Virginia

Patrick County Virginia: Postcards

Mount Airy, North Carolina

Martinsville, Virginia

Henry County Heritage Book Volume One

J. E. B. Stuart Birthplace: History, Guide, and Genealogy

Fieldale, Virginia

"If Thee Must Fight, Fight Well." William J. Palmer and the Fight for
Martinsville, April 8, 1865

Visit www.freestateofpatrick.com for more information

The Graham Mansion
A History and Guide

By Thomas D. Perry

ISBN-13: 978-1456353124
ISBN-10: 1456353128

Laurel Hill Publishing LLC
Owner, Thomas D. Perry
P. O. Box 11
4443 Ararat Highway
Ararat, VA 24053
www.freestateofpatrick.com
freestateofpatrick@yahoo.com

For Mary Lin Brewer, the lady of the house

About Thomas D. Perry

J. E. B. Stuart's biographer Emory Thomas describes Tom Perry as "a fine and generous gentleman who grew up near Laurel Hill, where Stuart grew up, has founded J. E. B. Stuart Birthplace, and attracted considerable interest in the preservation of Laurel Hill. He has started a symposium series about aspects of Stuart's life to sustain interest in Stuart beyond Ararat, Virginia." Perry holds a BA in History from Virginia Tech in 1983.

Perry started the J. E. B. Stuart Birthplace Preservation Trust, Inc. in 1990. The non-profit organization preserved 75 acres of the Stuart property including the house site where James Ewell Brown Stuart was born on February 6, 1833. Perry wrote the original eight interpretive signs about Laurel Hill's history along with the Virginia Civil War Trails sign and the new Virginia Historical Highway Marker in 2002. He spent many years researching traveling all over the nation to find Stuart materials including two trips across the Mississippi River to visit nearly every place "Jeb" Stuart served in the United States Army (1854-1861).

Tom can be seen on Virginia Public Television's Forgotten Battlefields: The Civil War in Southwest Virginia with his mentor noted Civil War Historian Dr. James I. Robertson, Jr. Perry has begun a collection of papers relating to Stuart and Patrick County history in the Special Collections Department of the Carol M. Newman Library at Virginia Tech under the auspices of the Virginia Center For Civil War Studies.

In 2004, Perry began the Free State Of Patrick Internet History Group, which has become the largest historical organization in the area with over 500 members. It covers Patrick County Virginia and regional history. Tom produces a monthly email newsletter about regional history entitled Notes From The Free State of Patrick that goes from his website www.freestateofpatrick.com.

In 2009, Perry used his book Images of America Henry County Virginia to raise over $25,000 for the Bassett Historical Center, "The Best Little Library in Virginia," and as editor of the Henry County Heritage Book raised another $30,000 of the $800,000 raised to expand the regional history library.

Contents

Acknowledgements

This book began in the 1980s when this author visited the Graham Mansion continuing a lifelong interest in J. E. B. Stuart and more importantly, an attempt to visit the places Stuart visited that still existed. Like many coming around the curve on Major Graham's Road Virginia Route 619, I was astounded to see the magnificent and huge structure residing on the high ground to my front. Over twenty years later, a discussion with Mary Lin Brewer led to the sharing of information and the start of a new project writing a history of the Graham Mansion.

The author would like to acknowledge the research of Nannie Tate Graham, local historians Davy Davis and Mary Kegley, Catherine S. McConnell and by Rick Graham, grandson of Major David Graham, who passed away in 1990.

Thanks to Jennifer Gregory, Debbie Hall, Mary Kegley, and Amy Snyder for reading the manuscript and making suggestions that improved the manuscript.

Introduction
Come Visit The Graham Mansion

This book is about history, but it is about a place full of history that you can visit. The Graham Mansion, owned today by Josiah C. Weaver, is home to many events throughout the year usually June through November including a music festival, a haunted house, a hunting preserve, seasonable public and private historical tours and the house is available for leasing for private events.

In 2012, the music will be at the St. Jude's GrahamFest carrying on the festival started by Josiah Weaver in partnership with WPSK and 100.7 Mix of Christiansburg and Pulaski, Virginia. Proceeds from this event will go to the St. Jude's Children's Hospital in Memphis, Tennessee.

Over the last four years numerous paranormal groups have visited the Graham Mansion and "yielded 100 EVPs (audio) clips, video recordings and other forms of measurable paranormal data." Beginning in 2011, the mansion and professional ghost hunters will offer paranormal investigations for the public. Come and see for yourself if the haunted mansion really is haunted.

If you like your haunting a little less real, but still scary the Graham Mansion is open each weekend in October for "SpookyWorld," which is described as a "wonderfully creepy studio type haunted mansion event." Each fall thousands of people come to Cedar Run to be scared.

The Graham Mansion is part of the W. W. Ranch, which offers guided hunts for white tail deer and spring gobbler hunts. In 2012, rainbow trout fishing, stream and lake, will begin.

Visit www.majorgrahammansion.com for more information.

PART ONE: HISTORY

Foreword
J. E. B. Stuart's Walk Through The Snow

On January 17, 1847, James Ewell Brown "Jeb" Stuart wrote to his cousin Alexander Brown from Draper's Valley in Pulaski County, Virginia. "I was disappointed in getting a horse here. So I set out on foot on Tuesday morning for Uncle Brown's I crossed the mountain and went up the back road by Graham's, where I dined upon quite a fine dinner, and then set out on my journey the snow being about half leg deep and I tell you that I had a tough time of it, for I had to break the road nearly all the way."

The house Stuart saw was not the large Graham Mansion visitors see today, but the wooden frame home built in the 1830s, tradition states, surrounding a cabin originally built by the Bakers in the 1780s. Construction of the brick home we see today began three years after Stuart's first visit along Cedar Run.

The future Confederate Major General was just one of many who visited the Graham Mansion in Wythe County, Virginia. His cousin, Alexander Stuart Brown, was the son of the man for whom he was named, Judge James Ewell Brown of Wytheville. Judge Brown was young Stuart's uncle, married to his paternal aunt, the sister of Stuart's father, Archibald Stuart.

Born on February 6, 1833, in Ararat, Patrick County, Virginia, on his parent's Laurel Hill Farm, Stuart was a few weeks shy of his fourteenth birthday when he visited the Grahams. He left the "Free State of Patrick" (Patrick County, Virginia) at age twelve promising his mother that he would not drink alcohol and came up Fancy Gap through Carroll County and across Thomas Jackson's Ferry on the New River. Stuart would fight a war with another man named Thomas "Stonewall" Jackson, but that was still over a decade in the future.

Stuart attended boy's schools in Wythe and nearby Pulaski County at the Draper's Valley home of Reverend George Painter and several in Wytheville including Mr. Buckingham's. Traveling between his school in Draper Valley and his Uncle Brown's home, Cobbler Springs, on the Pepper's Ferry Road near Wytheville brought young Stuart to the Graham home via the "back road." He came to the Graham home on December 22, 1847, on his way for Christmas celebration in Wytheville and not at his home the Laurel Hill Farm in Patrick County.

Stuart, known today as one of the most romantic figures from that war made famous from such films as Gone With The Wind, was truly a romantic young man. He wrote in the same letter of seeing Miss

Maria S. Crockett, "who was as fat and pretty as ever." He apparently was match making for his cousin Alexander Brown with Miss Crockett.

In 1845, James Stuart crossed the Blue Ridge to begin his formal education. He crossed the ferry on the New River like Caesar crossing a personal Rubicon. There are many reasons he made the journey including the lack of schools in Patrick County. The only reference to any school around Laurel Hill comes from oral tradition within the Pedigo family that an "Uncle John Mundey" taught a school for the local children including young James, but no further evidence exists. Stuart attended a boys' school run by attorney Peregrine Buckingham in Wytheville, Virginia. Buckingham, the son of Reverend Richard Buckingham, was born in 1822, and practiced law when not running the small school for boys. James Stuart also attended the music school operated by J.B. Wise and took voice lessons. There is evidence that Jeb's older brother, William Alexander Stuart, was present in Wythe County beginning his career that would make him the largest landowner in southwest Virginia.

On April 11, 1846, Stuart wrote to his cousin Alexander Stuart Brown that he was happy with Wytheville and had not been in a fight since he got there. Brown and Stuart's brother John were at Emory and Henry College. He noted that Archibald Stuart visited him and nearly caused a severe accident when he double loaded a rifle thinking it was unloaded. Young Stuart attracted the attention of several local young women and from his personal correspondence, it is clear that his time in Wythe County was an interesting one. Among the young ladies he mentions is Miss Maria S. Crockett (1829-1878), but his "luck with Cupid was all bad." Interestingly Maria married Dr. S. C. Gleaves (1823-1890), who became a surgeon for the Confederacy during the War Between the States. Stuart commented during this time, "I have gotten out with the girls. I believe they were just made for man's troubles." Stuart also mentions several places in his writing about his recreational activities near the New River.

He took time from his studies to visit the family of his uncle James Ewell Brown at Cobbler's Springs on the Pepper's Ferry Road. Judge Brown married Archibald Stuart's sister and their son as previously noted, Alexander Stuart Brown, corresponded for many years with J. E. B. Stuart.

The three years spent by Stuart in Wythe County included a sojourn in the Pulaski County community of Draper's Valley, where Stuart lived and studied at the Reverend George Whitfield Painter's home, Hillcrest. In a letter dated January 7, 1847, from Draper's Valley, Stuart said that Painter's place was "first rate" and that he "jogging away at old Caesar," but he would rather go to Mr. Buchannan's, another teacher in Wytheville. He commented that he wanted to go to "Patrick County in spring." Stuart got into a "scrape at Mr. Painter's" and returned to school with Buckingham and boarded at Mr. Miller's, but he made sure he told his cousin A. S. Brown that he was "not in love with Virginia Miller." One local story told by Frank Bowles, a recent owner of Hillcrest, was that the "scrape" involved Stuart staying out too late with one of the local girls. Her not very happy father came looking for the future general and the encounter ended Stuart's career in Pulaski County.

Stuart became sick with the measles or some ailment causing his hair to fall out. He recounts that all the girls found it very amusing. Stuart recuperated by going home to Patrick County. While James was visiting Laurel Hill in the winter of 1847-1848, the house burned down. Stuart wrote to his cousin Alexander Stuart Brown of the "sad disaster." He noted that his father and brother, John, were living in the kitchen, an outbuilding separate from the main house. In 1996, an archaeological excavation located the sites of the house and the kitchen.

A friend Stuart made in Wytheville was David French Boyd. Tradition holds that Boyd was engaged to Ellen Spiller, but when the engagement ended, he left Wythe County. Ellen Spiller eventually married Stuart's cousin Alexander S. Brown and later became the second wife of William Alexander Stuart.

David French Boyd and his brother Thomas Duckett Boyd (1854-1932) became members of the faculty at Louisiana State University and its predecessor the Seminary of Learning of the State of Louisiana, which was near Alexandria, Louisiana. The Superintendent before the Civil War was future Union General William T. Sherman.

During the war, Union forces captured Boyd twice. After the first capture, tradition holds that Sherman released him due to their pre-war friendship. When the war ended in 1865, the school reopened with D. F. Boyd as Superintendent. He remained at the school until 1880 when he resigned. Boyd went to Auburn University, but returned to LSU in 1884. Over the next fifteen years, David F. Boyd came and went at LSU before his death in 1899. Today, two buildings on campus bear the names of the Boyd brothers and the Boyd Professorships are the highest faculty rank at the home of the "Bayou Bengal Tigers." The nickname of the athletic teams comes from the Louisiana troops from Robert E. Lee's Army of Northern Virginia.

Boyd's manuscript in his papers at LSU titled *The Boyhood of J. E. B. Stuart* detail his friendship with Stuart. Boyd described his friend "Jim" or James Stuart as independent, sturdy, self-reliant, with energy, fortitude, rugged honesty and courage along with common sense. Boyd portrayed Stuart's focus and competitive nature describing a game of marbles, where Boyd says he never tried harder to win a fight than he did to win a game of marbles. He tells of Stuart's sense of humor when he got into a fight with a smaller quicker boy who grabbed Stuart by the hair and threw gravel about his head. Stuart feigned injury as he saw the schoolmaster approaching. Stuart grinned at his fighting partner from behind the schoolmaster as he took switches to Stuart's antagonist, who happened to be David F. Boyd.

Stuart's fun loving nature got him into trouble, but he made the most of it as Boyd described a whipping that Mr. Buckingham gave him was so minor that Stuart cried out "ludicrously" in pain. One story had Boyd and Stuart on top of a chicken coop in Wytheville one day studying Latin, when Stuart suddenly started dancing around the roof. He grabbed Boyd and gave him such a whirl that the latter fell off the building knocking him unconscious. Stuart leaped down regretting his action telling Boyd, "Oh, I didn't mean to do it. I wouldn't have hurt you for the world."

The Stuart connections in Wythe County continued after the Civil War including John Dabney Stuart living in the area. He rests today in the town cemetery across the street from Loretto, the home of William

Alexander Stuart. Today, a point of pride for those involved in Wythe County history involves the will of Stuart administered by William A. Stuart after his brother's death. The document resides in the Clerk of Court office in the Wythe County Court House in the Wythe County Will Book #10 page 664 dated September 12, 1865, with Flora Cooke Stuart and William Alexander Stuart under a $12,000 bond acting as administrators.

The year 1848 was momentous for young James Stuart. He, being the youngest son, had little prospect for inheritance and was bound for the military, the law or education. He wrote that, "I expect to teach school some when I leave here." Stuart worked with his brother William Alexander "Alick" for a time early in the year. He later claimed that he volunteered for service in the Mexican War, but he wrote authorities turned him down due to his youth. This is the first evidence that he was interested in a military career.

At age fifteen, James Stuart entered Emory and Henry College, where his cousin Alexander Stuart Brown and brother John Dabney Stuart attended from 1845 until 1847. According to proud alumnus, Eddie Wheeler of Roanoke, Virginia, this small school produced six Confederate Generals. They were William E. "Grumble" Jones, who attended from 1844 until 1846, James B. Gordon, who attended from

1841 until 1843 and who served under Stuart commanding the North Carolinians in the cavalry, Henry D. Clayton (1827-1889) of Georgia, William F. Tucker (1827-1881) of North Carolina and John C. Moore (1824-1910) of Tennessee.

The college began in 1836 and welcomed its first student two years later on the 150-acre campus. The Holston Conference of the United Methodist Church administers the oldest institution of higher learning in southwest Virginia. President Charles Collins of Maine and two other graduates of Wesleyan University in Connecticut made up the faculty. Reverend E. Langley taught Math and English. Reverend Ephraim Wiley, who became President in 1852, was the third along with Collins and Langley. His name adorns the large building that dominates the campus. During the Civil War, this building acted as a Confederate hospital. Also on campus during Stuart's time acting as Tutors or Adjuncts were George Everhart and the interestingly named William H. Faulkner.

For the first time in his life, an educational realm challenged Stuart and he met the challenge. He excelled in class and joined a debating society, the Hermesians. Stuart's education up to this time had been spotty beginning with tutoring by his mother and then beginning at twelve a variety of schools throughout Southwest Virginia in Wytheville and Pulaski. He entered as a special student still lacking in his studies, but in a show of dedication and discipline, he made up his deficiencies in his first year and entered his second year as a full sophomore. One contemporary described Stuart as being good in math and science and not a particularly good speaker.

Despite the heavy load of coursework, academics were not his only interest there. The best story of his time at Emory and Henry comes from Stuart himself and explains why he was not good on the lecture circuit. When he returned in 1859, he recounted that he gave a speech during his time on "Emory's college green." There was a young lady in the audience that he wished to impress so much that he lost his bearings and fell face first off the stage. Much to Stuart's "ever lasting mortification" he rose into a "storm of laughter" and much to his chagrin, the person laughing the hardest was the "sweetheart" he wished to impress.

The class sessions at Emory and Henry ran from August to January and February to July. Examinations were open to the public. The fees at Emory and Henry were fifteen dollars per session for tuition, fifty cents for library use, and one dollar and fifty cents for room and board.

Stuart read Ovid as a freshman in Latin class while at Emory and Henry along with Livy and Cicero. He was fluent in Latin and wrote to his former teacher Buckingham in Wytheville asking for a letter saying he had read the Aenead of Virgil. His first year included Greek, which involved translating such works as Xenophon along with algebra, bookkeeping, geometry, English including grammar, composition and elocution and history studying Rome and Greece with ancient geography.

Stuart's second year at Emory and Henry included Latin, Greek translating Herodotus and Plato, trigonometry, mensuration, surveying and navigation among the math with English including rhetoric, composition and elocution. There had been 129 or 164 students, depending on the source, in 1846. Being ten miles away from any town, the temptations of the big city were not present.

Stuart made many friends at Emory and Henry. Another classmate, John M. Davis, described Stuart as "generous to a fault, genial in disposition, and vivacious in spirit." Another, Drake Sanders, was the son of Hannah Walton Sanders and William John Sanders of Wythe County. Drake lived in Smyth County for a time but later moved back to Wythe County when he accepted a job at Walton Furnace. The Wytheville Enterprise recently featured the diary of his mother.

Stuart joined the Methodist Church while at Emory and Henry and spent the rest of his life trying to live a Christian's life. His father, Archibald Stuart, came from a long line of Presbyterians. His mother,

Elizabeth Letcher Pannill Stuart was a strict, religious, and disciplined woman with a loving nature. You can see many of these traits in her most famous offspring. Elizabeth was Episcopalian and local tradition holds that she attended services on Lebanon Hill in Mount Airy, North Carolina. This congregation formed Trinity Episcopal located on Main Street today.

Often overlooked is the spiritual of side of Stuart's life. In coming years, he founded a church in Kansas, bought his men copies of the scriptures from his own pocket, joined the Temperance Movement, and gave speeches about the temptation of alcohol. He never forgot where he came from as he sent his mother one hundred dollars and asked her to match it in order to start a church near Laurel Hill.

During his commencement, Stuart spoke of "The Triumph of True Principles." The night before he left, Stuart gave his friends a turkey dinner during which the president of the college, Charles Collins, came by to express his regrets at Stuart's departure. Collins wrote of Stuart's "irreproachably moral and social character."

With no prospects of inheriting a fortune from his father, his education in southwest Virginia was what today we might call prep school for an appointment to the United States Military Academy at West Point, New York. In 1850, Stuart received an appointment. He graduated in 1854, thirteenth in a class of forty-six, a class that lost more men in the Civil War than any other West Point class.

James Ewell Brown "Jeb" Stuart circa age 17 in 1850 at the United States Military Academy at West Point, New York.

Seven years in the U. S. Army followed, mainly in the Kansas Territory, before Stuart resigned in May 1861 and offered his sword to his native Virginia and then the newly formed Confederate States of America. He was first the Colonel of the First Virginia Cavalry in 1861 before rising to the rank of Major General in 1862 and command of all the cavalry in Robert E. Lee's Army of Northern Virginia.

Rising to the rank of Brigadier General after his performance at the Battle of First Manassas, Stuart led three separate raids around Union General George's McClellan's Army of the Potomac in 1862, near Richmond in June, after the Battle of Sharpsburg/Antietam, and just before the end of the year, the latter leading to Lincoln firing his commander.

Stuart replaced the wounded "Stonewall" Jackson commanding the latter's infantry corps at Chancellorsville in May 1863. Stuart at his zenith in 1863 commanded nearly 10,000 mounted men fighting one of the largest cavalry battles at Brandy Station in June. His controversial absence a month later for the first day and one half of the Battle of the Gettysburg is still felling trees for authors to write books.

Stuart died on May 12, 1864, after one of George Armstrong Custer's Michigan Cavalry gut shot him at the Battle of Yellow Tavern just north of Richmond, Virginia. Stuart rests today in that city's Hollywood Cemetery, far from his home in southwest Virginia.

Stuart's visit to the Graham Mansion was brief, but its influence was long bringing this author to the house in the 1980s for a visit, and this interest in the site led to this author's desire to write this book in 2010.

Stuart had other fleeting connections to the home from that already mentioned including two female members of his family such as a Mary Bell Peirce, who carved their initials and names in the second floor windows with their diamond engagement rings. Martha Peirce Graham, the wife of Squire David Graham, was the sister of James Peirce, who married Stuart's oldest sister Nancy Anne, making Martha and Nancy sisters-in-law and young James E. B. Stuart an extended member of the family.

Stuart was just one of the many interesting characters to visit or live at the Graham Mansion. This book is the story of many more who called the place home.

To Alexander Stuart Brown

From J. E. B. Stuart, Draper's Valley, Virginia
January 17, 1847

It is now dear cousin almost a month since I wrote to you last and I
resume my seat hoping that you will—View this not with a scornful eye
But pass its imperfections by. Although I have but little new to write yet
I hope that I will have something that will interest you.

I was disappointed in getting a horse here. So I set out on foot on
Tuesday morning for Uncle Brown's I crossed the mountain and went up
the back road by Graham's, where I dined upon quite a fine dinner, and
then set out on my journey the snow being about half leg deep and I tell
you that I had a tough time of it, for I had to break the road nearly all the
way.

I got to Cobbler Springs about sundown where I found Cousins T. and F.,
also Miss Mary McKee and Miss Maria S. Crockett who was as fat and
pretty as ever. I had the pleasure of riding home with her next morning
and in the conversation I brought up your name, and I talked about a
good many different things concerning you and found them to be o. k.
but away with this trash.

When I got there I found that I could not get a horse (I mean at Uncle
Brown's) until he arrived home which he did not until Thursday night
following. I thought it was not worth my while to go to Patrick County
until Spring at which time I intend to go or burst a gut.

I stayed there enjoying myself most remarkably well, until Tuesday
making a stay of just two weeks when accompanied with Miss Maria
Young I came down to the Valley where I have been ever since jogging
away at old Caesar

I suppose you've heard of the wedding etc. The Colonel has gone with a
carriage to Roanoke after his children. Things are going on about as
usual. I received a letter from Sister Columbia the other day. They were
all well and she requested me to send her love to you when I wrote to
you. My school will be out the last of March. I want to go home then and
stay until May and then go to Mr. Buckingham.

Yours, J. E. B. Stuart

Family Relationship Between Grahams, Peirces and Stuarts

Archibald and Elizabeth Letcher Pannill Stuart

    |
    |-Nancy Anne Dabney Stuart (1818-1846) married 1840
    Married James H. Peirce (son of David and Mary Bell Peirce)
        |
        |-Mary Bell Peirce married Dr. James Magill
        |-Elizabeth Pannill Peirce married George Litchfield
            |-Annie Stuart Litchfield married Rolfe Bolling
            (Rolfe is the brother of Mrs. Woodrow Wilson)
        |-David Stuart married Bettie Lawson Boyd
    |-Bethenia Pannill Stuart (1819-1910)
    |-Mary Tucker Stuart (1821-1888)
    |-David Pannill Stuart (1823-1845)
    |-William Alexander Stuart (1826-1892)
    |-John Dabney Stuart (1828-1877)
    |-Columbia Lafayette Stuart (1830-1857)
    |-James Ewell Brown Stuart married Flora Cooke
    (Confederate Major General J. E. B. Stuart 1833-1864)
    |-Unnamed infant (1834)
    |-Virginia Josephine Stuart (1836-1842)
    |-Victoria Augusta Stuart (1838-?)

David and Mary Bell Peirce

    |
    |-James Peirce married Nancy Anne Dabney Stuart
        |
        |-Mary Bell Peirce
    |-Martha Peirce married Squire David Graham

The first part of the mansion built in the 1830s possibly around the cabin built by the Baker Family in the late 1700s was the structure J. E. B. Stuart visited in 1847.

Chapter One
The Bakers

The river flowed in a new direction or at least that is one story on how the New River got its name. The irony is that the river is far from new, but one of the oldest bodies of flowing fresh water in the world. Cedar Run is one of the streams flowing into the Reed Creek, which makes its way to the New River. The New becomes the Kanawha before emptying into the Ohio River at Point Pleasant, West Virginia, and continuing on the Mississippi River and the Gulf of Mexico. On this small flowing water tributary, Cedar Run, the Graham Family came, but they were not the first.

Local history says William Mack, a Seventh Day Baptist or Dunkard, came down the Wilderness Road, paralleling what is today Highway 11 and Interstate 81, in 1745, and built a cabin on Reed Creek. Fifteen years later Fort Chiswell was built along the Wilderness Road, Warrior's Path or the road to Cumberland Gap depending on your interpretation. John Chiswell discovered lead and zinc and started a town with his brother-in-law Richard Byrd called Lead Mines.

John Chiswell prospected for minerals and his home in Williamsburg was a long way from Wythe County, Virginia, then Fincastle County. He discovered lead (galena) ore in the 1750s near the present day town of Austinville. His partners included Francis Fauquier, Royal Governor of Virginia, John Robinson, the treasurer of the Colony of Virginia and Colonel William Byrd of Westover and during the French and Indian War, they made musket balls. In 1761, Byrd on a relief mission to Fort Loudoun in Tennessee, built Fort Chiswell, which today is near the intersection of Interstates 77 and 81.

At the onset of the American Revolution, this area was Fincastle County. In 1775, the Fincastle Resolutions were a response to the British Parliament's "Intolerable Acts," a year before the Declaration of Independence and said the following.

"We are ready and willing to contribute all in our power for the support of his Majesty's Government, if applied to constitutionally, and when the grants are made by our own Representatives, but cannot think of submitting our liberty or property to the power of a venal British Parliament, or to the will of a corrupt Ministry.

We by no means desire to shake off our duty or allegiance to our lawful Sovereign, but on the contrary, shall ever glory in being the loyal subjects of a Protestant Prince, descended from such illustrious progenitors, so long as we can enjoy the free exercise of our Religion as Protestants, and our Liberties and Properties as British, subjects.

But if no pacifick measures shall be proposed or adopted by Great Britain, and our enemies will attempt to dragoon us out of those inestimable privileges, which we are entitled to as subjects, and to reduce us to a state of slavery, we declare that we are deliberately and resolutely determined never to surrender them to any power upon earth, but at the expense of our lives."

Thousands of settlers passed by the area on the way to the Cumberland Gap. Among them, the man Fess Parker made famous in the 1960s television show, Daniel Boone, who passed further to the west and into Kentucky.

Such begins the history of the Graham Mansion in southern Wythe County, Virginia. The county sits along the north bank of the New River in the Blue Ridge Highlands sandwiched between two states of North Carolina and West Virginia, with Carroll County, Virginia, acting as a buffer to the south and West Virginia with Bland County, Virginia, to the north.

Other families came to the area before the Grahams including two brothers from Philadelphia, Pennsylvania, Moses and Stephen Austin (1780-1800). The former had a son he named Stephen F. Austin, who became the "Father of Texas" being one of many from Virginia like Sam Houston who made their way to the Lone Star State. Moses Austin moved to Missouri in 1800 leaving his nephew Charles in Philadelphia to rent the lead mines.

Iron and lead brought many of these people to the area and provided them a livelihood. Thomas Jackson, whose family owned the ferry J. E. B. Stuart crossed in the 1850s was in the business with partners Daniel Sheffey and David Peirce. Jackson built the Shot Tower in the early 1800s on land bought from Moses Austin. The seventy-five foot limestone tower with walls two feet thick had a furnace room at the top with a shaft that gravity carried the lead to a kettle of water at the bottom. The furnace melted the lead and it was poured through a sieve to separate it into droplets that fell into the kettle of water. The size of the shot depended on the mesh in the sieve. The lead shot was "recovered, sorted, polished, and shipped."

Thomas Jackson was born in Westmoreland County, England, in 1762. Jackson arrived in the area circa 1785-90 and began blacksmithing in Austinville. Jackson outbid a Captain James Newel, who got the rights from the Austin family for the mines. Jackson and David Peirce experienced problems and Jackson went downstream and built the Shot Tower.

Thomas Jackson died in 1824. His nephews, Michael and Robert Jackson, took over the operation. In 1835, they leased to other nephews,

Robert Raper and John Jackson, who worked the site for six years. Beginning in 1843, the Wythe Lead Mines Company rented the site for five years. The Jackson Family owned the site until 1929 when M. H. Jackson donated it to the Daughters of the American Revolution. From 1952 until 1964, the Lead Mines Ruritan Club operated the historic site. The Commonwealth of Virginia made the Shot Tower a State Park in 1964. The American Society of Mechanical Engineers made the site an Engineering Landmark in 1980.

The lead mines in Austinville were the source of income for the area and the object of destruction for Union cavalry in the Civil War. Minerals such as iron and lead would dominate the economy for over two hundred years. The last operation belonged to New Jersey Zinc Company, who closed operations in 1981.

Colonel James White of Abingdon was one of many who came to the area. Another was David Peirce, born in Chester County, Pennsylvania, who came to Poplar Camp in 1756 along present day Interstate 77 and got an interest in the lead mines. He was a Friend or Quaker and went into the iron manufacturing business. This interest eventually belonged to the Grahams through marriage into the Peirce family when Squire David Graham married David Peirce's daughter, Martha.

In 1777, this area became Montgomery County. In 1779, George Shillideay sold 198 acres to Joseph Baker along Cedar Run. Many local historians report that the frame section of the Graham Mansion was built in 1785 around a log cabin owned by Joseph Baker.

The local story has it that Joseph Baker and two of his slaves, Bob and Sam, were making moonshine "out back." Baker told the slaves that in his will he would give them their freedom upon his death. The slaves hastened Baker's untimely demise..." Whether drinking or an argument or both along with the promise of freedom through murder caused the assault is not known, but often suspected.

In the Montgomery Courthouse, there is a record of the sheriff arresting Bob and Sam, their subsequent trial, and their hanging. There is also a record of the sheriff being paid 200 lbs. of tobacco for his efforts in 1786.

Local lore has it that Bob and Sam's spirits "still roam the hills surrounding Cedar Run." One tradition has the Sheriff hung Bob and Sam from a hickory tree on the hill overlooking the mansion and buried the slaves there, but according to court documents they were "probably" hung at Fort Chiswell and their burial place is unknown.

John Baker inherited the land on which the Graham Mansion sits today. Other records show that in 1787 James and Rebecca Tuttle moved to Wilkes County, Georgia, and sold 400 acres to John Baker. This land became Wythe County in 1790 named for the mentor of Thomas Jefferson, George Wythe. In 1793, Baker sold 187 acres to Daniel Miller. The land came to the Crockett family next and from them the land along Cedar Run came to the Graham Family.

Squire David Graham

Chapter Two
Squire David Graham

Robert Graham, the father of Squire David Graham, came from County Down, Ireland, to North America in 1774, just before the American Revolution. There is some evidence that he lived for a "short time in Pennsylvania and South Carolina. He moved to Sugar Creek in Mecklenburg County, North Carolina, by April 1778, when he bought 170 acres in two tracts on Sugar Creek for 60 pounds. In July 1778, he bought 145 acres between McMichael's and Sugar Creeks, both from Thomas Polk, a relative of future President of the United States James K. Polk. On April 20, 1779, he bought 200 acres on Sugar Creek from William Walker. In 1781, he served as executor of the estate of James Walker."

Robert came to the Locust Hill area of what is now Wythe County from North Carolina in 1782 settling on what eventually became nearly 1,300 acres. One writer said, "The Grahams were in Pennsylvania, but the soil was too hard. The Grahams came to North Carolina, but the soil was too soft which brought them to Virginia, where the soil was just right."

Tradition states Robert served one year in the American Revolutionary War and was father to seven children from his first wife,

Mary Craig, and eight by his second wife, Mary Cowan. Robert Graham was a gimlet maker, (a small hand tool for drilling small holes, mainly in wood, without splitting) a preacher, and operated an "ordinary" or tavern in what was then Montgomery County.

He was the first Elder of Anchor of Hope Presbyterian Church in Max Meadows. The name comes from paraphrased from a Bible passage "anchor of hope in Ye Valley of contention and strife." In 1828, Reverend George Painter pastored the church, while he ran the school for boys at his home Hillcrest in Draper's Valley. J. E. B. Stuart was among his students.

David Graham, the man we call "Squire" was born on September 3, 1800. His father died when he was 10 or 11 years old. Joseph McGavock, Jr., husband of Squire's half-sister, Margaret Graham, became guardians of young David Graham and his siblings, older half-brothers, James and Samuel Graham. Joseph's nephew, the son of James McGavock, built the Fort Chiswell mansion near the intersections of Interstates 77 and 81. Squire's mother passed when he was 19.

At age 26, Squire David purchased 2000 acres in twelve tracts, various iron-making buildings, and a furnace on Reed Creek and Cedar Run from the Crockett heirs (James and Andrew) and John Baker for $10,000. This purchase included a 213-acre tract on Cedar Run on what today most people call the Major David Graham Mansion, but it is misnamed. It should be called the Squire David Graham Mansion in honor of the Major's father. For this book I refer to it as the Graham Mansion as the house is really a building built by father and son with the same name.

Squire David built the original house and the majority of the later additions. The original, rear wooden frame section of the Mansion was built in the 1830s possibly around the log structure of the Bakers and the huge, formal brick section was added in the 1850s.

The Graham Mansion was built in four stages, two under the direction of Squire David Graham (1838 and 1855) and two under his son's direction (1870 and 1890). In 1848, bricks made locally went into another major Mansion "addition." By 1855-56, another major Mansion "addition" included a 45 foot square by 40-foot high brick structure. We know this because there is a substantial increase in value on property tax paid in 1840, which indicates additions to the large building.

Squire David Graham married Martha Bell Peirce of nearby Poplar Camp, Virginia, on December 15, 1835. Born on February 2, 1806, she was the daughter of David and Mary Bell Peirce. They lived first at Boiling Springs, where they buried two infants before he brought her to the "Cedar Run Farm." Their "often stormy union" produced many children, although two died as infants as previously stated before 1837.

The couple had five surviving children. David Graham (1838-1898) married Nannie Montgomery Tate, the daughter of Charles Campbell Tate and Elizabeth Friel. Major David Graham, the first born surviving child, served in the War Between the States and inherited the mansion from his father Squire David Graham. Robert Calving Graham (1841-1852) died young. Mary Bell Graham (1843-1900) married H. J. Matthews. Elizabeth Ann Graham (1845-1921) married John W. Robinson, who became a business partner with his brother-in-law, Major David Graham. Emily Maria Graham (1848-1889) married J. W. McGavock and was the last child of Martha and Squire David Graham.

Squire David Graham was a big part of his community for several decades. He was a Justice of the Peace in 1826. That same year he acquired a "license for a house of private entertainment." He was a Trustee of Methodist Brick Church in 1837 as his wife was a Methodist. He was Presbyterian and founded Galena Presbyterian Church in 1850. He even managed to get his face on a $10 bill from the South Western Bank of Wytheville.

By 1860, Squire David Graham accumulated 6,000 acres of land. His "real property" was worth $70,000 and included as many as fourteen iron furnaces along with forges, gristmills, rolling mills, nail works, and even a general store.

Squire David Graham

That same year, 1860, an interesting exchange between Squire David Graham and Reverend W. H. Bates occurred when on returning from Richmond Graham wrote the preacher the following on September 22.

"I was very much surprised to learn that during my absence, you had entered my family and baptized all my children, without ever having consulted me upon the subject, or without my knowing anything about it, from any other source.

It is no apology to say, that my wife asked you to perform this service. I am the head of the family and as such should have been consulted, and permit me to say that no gentleman would have assumed that responsibility without consulting me."

The Reverend responded from Newbern, Pulaski County, Virginia, four days later stating, "a thunder peal in a clear sky would not have surprised me more." Squire David Graham shows in this letter that he is somewhat paranoid about religious matters and there was obviously some trouble between Squire and Mrs. Graham.

In 1860, Graham employed 29 slaves of his own and hired dozens more from other owners to operate his many operations. Slave labor supported the Southern agricultural economy, but also the industrial economy of the region.

The Small Special Collections Library at the University of Virginia houses the papers on the Graham, Tate, and Sanders families containing twenty ledger books and over 3,000 papers document the business interests of Squire and Major David Graham including books on their slaves. In June 1830, as an example, the "Slave Book" lists the names of those held in bondage as Carter, Charles, Isaac, Phil, Duke,

Dennis, Jack, Will, Buck, Terry, Caesar, Randal, George, Ben, Lewis, Sam, Peter, Adam, Rueben, Matt, Bryer, Church, Terry, Hardin and Bill.

Graham, known as the "first ironsmith of southwest Virginia," was part owner of the nearby Wythe Union Lead Mines, which he purchased for $8,000 in 1853 from William and Alexander Peirce including 1,400 acres. Graham was a Director of the Virginia and Tennessee Railroad. Squire David Graham built an iron furnace just down the road from the Mansion. Pig iron from the Graham forges went by horse-drawn wagon to larger cities and tradition states then it went overseas to England.

He produced iron products such as large salt kettles for the saltworks in Saltville, stoves, nails, plates, pipes, rails, hobbles for horses, fire backs, and iron for cannons for at least forty-four years and possibly fifty years.

One writer describes the tenacity of Squire David Graham this way. "David was very stubborn. Some other men, perhaps brothers were interested in buying an iron furnace. They left by horse for Richmond to buy the furnace. David had his wife to pack a sack of corn meal, went to the smoke house got a side of meat, with his sack he set out for Richmond on foot. He got to Richmond, bought the iron furnace, and started back home and arrived home before the other men even got to

Richmond. The other men had stopped at Taverns to rest

David would go by horse to check the furnaces, all 13 of them, and come

home walking; he would send someone out next morning to bring the

horse home."

Evidence exists that his father, Robert Graham, was involved in

the iron making business in North Carolina before coming to what is

today Wythe County. His growing tavern and business interests were the

foundation on which Squire David Graham built his wealth. When the

young man was twenty-one, ten years after his father's death one local

writer told, "waggoners and horsemen stopped at Graham's house for

entertainment and Graham was never known to be out of money."

The first of Graham's furnaces originally called "Parry Mount"

or Paramount were located three miles southeast of Graham's Forge.

Abandoned in 1832, the second Paramount operated for another twenty

years between Graham's Forge and Barren Springs. Graham owned the

Barren Spring cold blast charcoal furnace built in 1854. Graham's Forge

on Reed Creek built in 1800 and rebuilt in 1856 was under the same roof

with a rolling mill. By 1881, it was the only forge left in Wythe County

and operated until 1916 when a flood on Reed Creek destroyed it. Today

a gristmill sits on the site.

Squire David Graham tried to get transportation improved to his industrial sites. In 1826 and nine years later, he petitioned the local court to change the roads to pass by his furnace and make a road to North Carolina.

Squire David Graham lived until 1870, but the last ten years of his life were caught up in the great conflagration that was war. Whether you call it Civil War or the War Between the States, the "great scourge of war" affected his life and that of his children in ways they could not have imagined in 1860.

Squire David Graham wrote his will on February 8, 1870. In the document, he left 3,600 acres to his son David, 1,700 acres to daughter Elizabeth Robinson, 818 acres to daughter Mary Matthews and 1,500 acres to daughter Emily. He divided his interest in the lead mines with 1/3 to his son and the remaining 2/3 to his daughters collectively.

When Squire David Graham passed on October 16, 1870, at Cedar Run Farm, the Wytheville Dispatch had this to say about him. "The whole country and district of Southwest Virginia will feel affected with this information, as he was so well and so favorably known. The name of David Graham was in all the public enterprises of the district, in which he took a large and lively interest. His advice, his skill and his experience were sought on almost every occasion of importance, and his counsels were widely beneficial to his neighbors and his friends. In his own proper department of industry, he had no compeer (a person of equal status) in the district. He commanded the greatest success, producing the best material, and his brand of iron is so generally known and sought after, that he realized for it the highest market price from season to season. He had a correct knowledge of the quality and value of ores, and his selection of them proved his sound experience. He was distinguished by thoughtful action, by true friendship, and by Christian integrity, and there is in his case a certain hope of a resurrection until life eternal. A very large concourse attended his funeral and attested the high esteem in which he was held. May he ever rest in peace."

Martha Peirce Graham is a mysterious figure. The wife of Squire David and mother of Major David Peirce Graham suffered from mental illness documented in her daughter Elizabeth's journal from just before and during the first few years of the Civil War.

There is evidence that Squire David Graham imprisoned his wife in a basement room. "Her signature can be found on one of the basement shackle room doors, where it is believed she was locked away when guests came to visit the family." Martha Peirce Graham died on October 22, 1865, during the war. Such was the sad ending for the mistress of the Graham mansion.

Her successor, her daughter-in-law, would have a much better life at the home she and her husband Major David Peirce Graham lived. Nancy "Nannie" Montgomery Tate faced hardships due to war and experienced loss, but she would leave this world having raised her children and experienced a good life in the Graham Mansion. To her credit, her tenure at the mansion on Cedar Run comes down to us as a "Happy House."

Elizabeth Anne "Bettie" Graham Robinson

Chapter Three
The Coming War

In 1861, Major David Peirce Graham joined the armies of the Confederate States of America. With his future brother-in-law John Robinson, he formed a company in the 51st Virginia Infantry. Another chapter covers his civilian life after the war, but this one and the following chapter contain his family's experiences and his regiment, the 51st Virginia Infantry's history in the war.

Like many young men from the South, David P. Graham had some military training. He spent exactly one year and one month as a Keydet at the Virginia Military Institute in Lexington, Virginia, where he most certainly had Thomas J. Jackson as a teacher. The future "Stonewall" Jackson, considered one of the worst teachers in the history of the school, became one of the most famous commanders of the War Between the States. Graham resigned from "The Institute" stating, "when discipline becomes tyranny, resistance become duty."

Elizabeth Ann Graham or "Bettie" was David P. Graham's sister. Her diary, kept during the Civil War, reveals much about the Graham home life and the times. The *Journal of Bettie Ann Graham, October 18, 1860 – June 21, 1862* is published and housed in the Special Collections of the University of Virginia Library.

Elizabeth "Bettie" Ann Graham was 450 miles away from the Graham Mansion in Wythe County when Abraham Lincoln's election in November 1860 started a chain of events that led to war five months later in April 1861 with the firing on Fort Sumter in Charleston Harbor, South Carolina. Over the next four Aprils, war changed many lives in the extended Graham Family. Bettie was in Philadelphia, Pennsylvania, with her sister Mary at a "fashionable boarding school for girls." She began her journal on Thursday, October 18, 1860, at 1323 Spruce Street, with a somewhat foreboding passage about the impending crisis facing the nation. "Today I knew my lessons well. I believe I got perfect on them all, but I did not have but two. Arithmetic and Physiology. This morning we were very much delighted at the site of a military company passing up Spruce. I always experience a peculiar sensation when I see a military company."

Abraham Lincoln defeated three other candidates on Tuesday, November 6, 1860. The next day Bettie wrote, "Well, I believe Lincoln is elected at last, but I hope the consequences will not be as woeful as has been anticipated by many. There was very little excitement among the girls, in general, but a few seemed to think the election depended on their exertions." The next day she noted, "I wonder if we will go home to the South, now that Lincoln is elected."

On December 17, 1860, Bettie and her sister Mary received a letter from their father, Squire David Graham stating, "he was afraid we would not be able to remain here two years and perhaps not even this year out." She also received a letter from Nannie Tate.

Nancy "Nannie" Montgomery Tate was born on February 8, 1843. The child of Charles Campbell Tate and Elizabeth Friel Graham, the latter the daughter of James Graham and Nancy Montgomery. Nannie was the future Mrs. David P. Graham and sister of brothers who fought in the war. This family too felt the experiences of war being "touched by fire" and sadly knowing the loss that so many felt due to the Civil War.

William Hanson Tate, born September 19, 1837, in Wythe County, the brother of Nannie Montgomery Tate Graham, joined the 51st Virginia Infantry, serving as a First Lieutenant from July 31, 1861, until July 8, 1864, when he received promotion to Captain. He, like Graham, was at VMI for one year in 1857, after one year at nearby Washington College (1855-56), which became Washington and Lee College after the war. William taught school before the war. Dr. James I. Robertson of Virginia Tech often talks of the profession of teacher being dominated by males before the war and thereafter became the realm of females, who to this day dominate one of the hardest and most important jobs in the world.

James Graham Tate, born in 1840, another brother of the future Nannie Tate Graham, joined Captain William Terry's Company of "Wythe Grays," the 4th Virginia Infantry, after studying at Emory and Henry College. Twins, Thomas L. Tate and Charles Bentley Tate, born February 18, 1847, also served in the war. Thomas attended VMI before resigning. He became part of the 4th Virginia Reserves rising to the rank of Captain of Company G.

Rumors of war became rampant in the months after Lincoln's election. At that time, the President did not take the oath of office until March and not January 20 as we do today. Therefore, the nation waited four months before Lincoln came to power. This gave the states of the Deep South time to take action. On December 20, South Carolina became the first state to secede from the Union. Two days earlier Bettie Graham wrote in her journal, "I heard today...that Buchanan had resigned and that Breckenridge had taken the presidential chair, the place which I wish it was his to occupy for the next four years. 'Dissolution of the Union' Oh! Horrible thought; our glorious country would then be a reproach, and something for other countries to rejoice over. Our government is certainly the most perfect ever devised by human minds, and to think of the resting places of those noble men who achieved this glorious liberty for us being overrun by the blood of the citizens of the United States and spilled by their brothers."

James Buchanan, the fifteenth President of the United States and considered by most historians to be one of the worst mainly due to his inaction during the secession crisis of 1860-61, did not resign nor did his Vice-President John Breckenridge of Kentucky, who was a candidate against Lincoln in the 1860 election succeed him. Breckenridge became a Confederate General and led members of the extended family at the Battle of New Market in May 1864 with tragic consequences.

War came in 1861 to Wythe County. J. E. B. Stuart resigned from the U. S. Army on May 10, 1861, at Cairo, Illinois, where the Ohio and Mississippi Rivers collide. Stuart like Julius Caesar nearly two millennia before crossed another Rubicon as he had the New River all those years ago. He wrote of getting some men from Wythe County together to form a unit for the experienced Stuart to lead.

As things were coming to a head, Bettie Graham in Philadelphia wrote on February 8, "General Chapman came today; he called for us and said Pa told him to make arrangements for taking us home if need be." By this date, Alabama, Florida, Georgia, Louisiana, and Mississippi joined South Carolina in secession from the United States. Within days,

Texas would join them and the next day Mississippian Jefferson Davis became the provisional President of the Confederate States of America.

On March 4, 1860, Lincoln's inauguration occurred in Washington with the new President finishing his address with these words. "In your hands, my dissatisfied fellow-countrymen, and not in mine, is the momentous issue of civil war. The Government will not assail you. You can have no conflict without being yourselves the aggressors. You have no oath registered in heaven to destroy the Government, while I shall have the most solemn one to "preserve, protect, and defend it. I am loath to close. We are not enemies, but friends. We must not be enemies. Though passion may have strained it must not break our bonds of affection. The mystic chords of memory, stretching from every battlefield and patriot grave to every living heart and hearthstone all over this broad land, will yet swell the chorus of the Union, when again touched, as surely they will be, by the better angels of our nature."

Two weeks later Bettie wrote in her journal of ominous news from home that "there had been an insurrection among the negroes down there." No doubt, this rumor came from the possibility of freedom with the new President. This speaks to the paranoia that Southerners felt over their "peculiar institution."

She wrote on April 15, "There seem to be great excitement in town today. There was quite a mob raised this afternoon; having heard that General Patterson was a secessionists they were going to pull down his house, until he hung out the Union flag. There is no telling where all this excitement will end; I hope not in all this glorious company being involved in war." Three days earlier she reported that there had "almost been a quarrel and fight tonight among the Northerners and Southerners, and ended by Mrs. Cary sent out to get some ice cream." She could not know that very evening in Charleston, South Carolina, war started with the bombardment of Fort Sumter by Southerners.

Abraham Lincoln called for volunteers to put down the "rebellion." The next day Bettie wrote, "I have heard that Virginia has seceded. Indeed I don't care what she does now, I feel perfectly indifferent." It was actually the next day, April 17 that Virginia's Secession Convention vote to secede followed over the next month by Tennessee, Arkansas, and finally North Carolina, first in flight on their license plates today and last in secession.

Feeling more isolated in Philadelphia, Bettie wrote on the 19th, "I hear this morning that Virginia has seceded, and that all slaves are rising in rebellion and that all the men have to stay home and keep them down. Oh! It is terrible, too terrible! To think of. I wish almost that I could never hear of these horrid affairs, but so it must be." Three days later she wrote, "Oh! I feel as if I never was to see home again. If I could only be there once more. If they are doomed to death let me die with them, I pray."

Bettie is not unusual in her thoughts. Hysteria like this and false rumors no doubt led to the beginning of the war, but she did not have long to wait as her savior was on his way to rescue her. She wrote on Saturday, April 27, "We received a note from Pa this morning saying that he arrived last night and would be up early and if we could would like to start about eleven o'clock for home." Even with war looming over them the Graham girls went to the "swimming school and Dr. Jenkins." Squire David Graham was not amused. "Pa became so excited and impatient that he went out and did not return until it was so late that we missed the car."

Bettie, Mary, and Squire David Graham left Philadelphia heading home for Wythe County, Virginia, on Sunday, April 28. The next day as they waited on the Susquehanna River at Harve de Grace to pass through Maryland, the state rejected secession and thus did not isolate the U. S. Capitol in Washington by surrounding it with seceded states.

With all the excitement, traveling home was more difficult than Bettie liked describing it as "the longest day I've ever spent in my life and I hope it will be my last at Havre de Grace…what's more I don't want to be." They reached Baltimore on April 30 and made it to Harper's Ferry, Virginia then, West Virginia now, by 9 a.m. on May 1. Bettie noted, "There is a company upon the mountain watching out for the enemy. The bridge of which old John Brown took possession is about ten steps from me." By afternoon, the Grahams transferred to "a stage with six other persons…and eleven on top."

Their trip home continued through Manassas Junction on May 2. The next day, "We stopped at Lynchburg and washed our faces and had dinner." She noted a large number of troops from Kentucky, which remained in the Union.

On May 5, 1861, Bettie Graham was home, but it was not home sweet home. She noted in her journal. "Tis as I expected. Nothing but quarrelling all the time. I pray that none I love may ever know the pangs inflicted by a drunken father and an insane mother. How I idolize my brother none can know."

At the Graham Mansion in southern Wythe County, war came calling as well, but not immediately. Company B was from Wythe County under David Peirce Graham, the brother Bettie so idolized. Company B, the Wharton Grays, originally Company H enlisted July 31, 1861, for one year. This unit joined the 51st Virginia Regiment on August 14, 1861. Grahams serving in the regiment were A. J., David Peirce, Jackson, James, Noah B., Parris M., and Zaccheus.

At Camp Jackson in Wytheville, the Grahams joined the companies of the 51st Regiment of Virginia Infantry under the command of an 1847 graduate of the Virginia Military Institute and civil engineer, Gabriel C. Wharton. Born in Culpeper, Virginia, Wharton graduated second in his class at the VMI. Practicing Civil Engineering in Arizona before the war, he became a major in the 45th Virginia in July 1861 and then Colonel of the 51st Virginia Infantry.

Joining the first commander, Colonel Gabriel C. Wharton, were the Field Officers of the 51st Virginia Infantry including Major William T. Akers, Major George A. Cunningham, Major Stephen M. Dickey, Lt. Colonel Augustus Forsberg, Major David P. Graham, Lt. Colonel James W. Massie, Lt. Colonel Samuel H. Reynolds, Lt. Colonel John P. Wolfe, and Major William A. Yonce.

Men from all over southwest Virginia joined the regiment under "Old Gabe." The men were from Wythe, Grayson, Wise, Patrick, Nelson, Bland, Tazewell, Amherst, and Floyd Counties. The 51st Virginia Infantry Regiment organized in Wytheville during August 1861 with ten companies, A thru K. Company L enlisted on August 22, 1861, and was assigned to the 23rd Battalion Virginia Infantry in January 1862.

Two companies (C and F) from Patrick County joined their fellow Virginians in the regiment. According to all available records at least 391 men from the county served in this unit. More Patrick Countians served in the 51st Regiment of Virginia Infantry than in any other regiment. The companies from Patrick County formed in June 1861. One group became Company C under David Lee Ross. Ninety-seven men drilled on his farm on present-day Highway 57 near the intersection with Pole Bridge Road. Captain Ross served as an officer in the county militia before the war. Other officers included William Tyler Akers, Abner J. Harbour, and Charles F. Ross serving as lieutenants in Company C. This unit enlisted on June 14, 1861, for one year. They reorganized May 5, 1862 with Captains David Lee Ross until April 1862, William T. Akers, who became a Major in 1864 and Rufus J. Woolwine.

Rufus James Woolwine of the 51st Virginia Infantry Regiment saw many important places and events throughout the war. Not only did he live to tell about it, he kept notes during his time in the army.

The Patrick County community of Woolwine gets its name from Rufus's father, the first postmaster, Thomas Woolwine. Sarah Adams Woolwine, his mother, was the daughter of Notley P. Adams. Rufus James Woolwine, born October 20, 1840, attended the common schools and went to work with his father as a saddler. He enlisted on June 14, 1861 as a private and mustered in as a fourth corporal on July 26.

Another group called the "Blackhawk" company organized under Granville P. Conner at Davis Shop on the Smith River in Patrick County. This unit was originally designated as Company F with William G. Price, John M. Cruise, and Nathan B. Terry as lieutenants. They enlisted on July 2, 1861, for one year. They reorganized on May 23, 1862, with Captains Granville R. Conner and William G. Price, who was wounded and captured.

Both Patrick County companies drilled until July 24, 1861, then marched to Christiansburg where they boarded a train on the Virginia and Tennessee Railroad for Wytheville.

Augustus Forsberg wrote of them at this time, "It was interesting to notice the personnel of the volunteer-like mountaineers, they were courageous, fine physical development, and could compare with any troops on earth…Some in uniforms they had made at home, some with squirrel rifles, some with flint locks and Bowie knifes. Some had never seen a railroad. Once the sound of a locomotive was heard and the men acted like being shocked, one called out 'She's a coming', down went all guns and like a flock of sheep, ran down the hill to see the Iron Horse."

Born in Sweden in 1832, Forsberg served as a Swedish Army Engineer before coming to America in the 1850s. He rose in rank to Colonel and command of the 51st Virginia Infantry Regiment in 1863.

After having dinner at Gabriel DeHart's home on Rock Castle Creek at the foot of Tuggle's Gap, Rufus Woolwine wrote in his diary on July 24, "The scene of parting is a day that can never be described, never be forgotten. Twas then we bid farewell to home, friends, and connections and took up the lines of march to meet the serried ranks of a strong but dastard foe. Twas then many of us looked upon our native soil as we thought for the last time." Upon arriving at Christiansburg, their accommodations caused Woolwine to write, "Landed there about one o'clock in the night and I do assure you that our feathers fell when they lighted us to our stall... What we were furnished with there over night discouraged several so they laid in an excuse and plead for a discharge."

Young men going off to war inspired Captain Ross' black servant, Britt, to poetry.

"The twenty fourth of July, may long remember be,
The volunteers from Patrick the men to march away,
The patriotic spirit induces them to go,
To meet the Northern plunders and keep them from the shore.
A true hearted soldier he stands at his post,
In danger he's never found out of his course
He's willing to fight if it's five to their ten
Lord aid Captain Ross and all his brave men.
Lord aid our captain while we are in camp,
Grant every man to have oil in his lamp,
and be ready if called on with a load to depart,
with a beautiful beed on a northern man's heart.
Here's health to the poet that did make the song,
his life to be merry, his day's to be long,
good luck to all our soldier's that live under the sun,
success to Captain Ross and all his brave Patrick men."

 Gabriel Wharton

 David Lee Ross commanded a company from
Patrick County in the 51st Virginia Infantry. *Courtesy of Paul Ross.*

In studying the Civil War, focusing on battles or leaders and forgetting about the ordinary infantry soldier is commonplace. In Patrick County, the same is true for James Ewell Brown "Jeb" Stuart. You see his name and image everywhere, but there were many infantry soldiers who fought in the war and deserve recognition.

Company K, the "Bland Tigers," enlisted June 26, 1861, for one year. They reorganized on May 20, 1862, with Captains Samuel H. Newberry, who was not re-elected, but reappointed on May 29, 1863, and William G. Repass, who resigned on February 6, 1863.

Company G, the "Floyd Gamecocks," also known as Floyd Game Bucks, enlisted on June 29, 1861, for one year. They reorganized on July 1, 1861 with Captain James William Henry.

Companies A and D from Grayson County organized under Stephen M. Dickey and Ezekiel Young. Company A enlisted on June 24, 1861, for one year. They reorganized on May 6, 1862, with Captains Stephen Mills Dickey, who became a Major on May 26, 1862, William A. Cooper, who resigned on January 25, 1865.

Company D enlisted on June 28, 1861, for one year. They reorganized on May 23, 1862, with Captains Ezekiel Young, Calvin H. Senter, who resigned in 1862, and William C. Bourn, who was wounded in 1864.

Company E, the "Wythe Rifles," enlisted on July 20, 1861, for one year. They reorganized May 3, 1862 with Captains William H. Cook, William A. Yonce, who became a Major on April 23, 1864), and Jehiel F. Umbarger.

Company B, the "Nelson County Rifles," enlisted July 1, 1861, for one year. They reorganized on May 7, 1862, with Captains: John Turner Dillard to April 1862, Thomas J. Graves, who resigned in 1862, and Austin J. Graves, who resigned in 1863, and Josephus Mills.

Company I contained men from Washington County under Captain John P. Wolfe. They became Company A after enlisting on July 16, 1861, for one year. They reorganized May 20, 1862 with Captains: John P. Wolfe and Daniel Hoge Bruce.

Company L enlisted on August 22, 1861, and was assigned to the 23rd Battalion Virginia Infantry in January 1862. They were the last unit to join the 51st, Company L, hailed from Tazewell County.

The men listened to its eleven-piece regimental band. Burton Highley watched over the spiritual health of the men as minister of the regiment and James Estill performed the duties of regimental surgeon.

The companies came together due to Brigadier General John B. Floyd's need for troops in the Kanawha Valley, in present-day West Virginia. In August 1861, the regiment took the train to Bonsack Depot, just east of present-day Roanoke, and camped from August 5 until September 19. The regiment moved to the Kanawha Valley in present-day West Virginia in early September leaving the two Patrick companies behind. The men from Patrick rejoined the regiment after about three weeks. An epidemic of measles broke out in the two Patrick companies. Two men, James Ross and Robert Hodges, from Company D died from measles.

The First Battle of Manassas occurred on July 21, 1861, with a rousing Southern victory and propelling Thomas J. Jackson to the legend of "Stonewall" Jackson. The reader will note that David P. Graham did not raise men until ten days after the battle continuing to be cautious that war might be avoided.

In the two months since arriving home from Philadelphia, Bettie Graham continued to keep her journal. She wrote on May 7. "Ma does not seem to be in her right mind at all today. She takes up the strangest ideas I have ever heard of; she's got it into her head that Cousin Laura is a rogue and steals all her eggs, brandy and sugar, and that she is going to have a child. Poor Cousin Laura! She is so innocent and unsuspecting." Two days later she wrote, "Cousin Bell is coming down next week; I never wanted to see anybody so badly in my life as I do her for I love her oh! so dearly." This is probably Mary Bell Peirce, the niece of J. E. B.

Stuart and daughter of James and Nancy Anne Dabney Stuart Peirce.
Mary Bell Peirce's signature is carved into the upstairs bedroom in the
Graham Mansion.

On May 23, Virginia's people voted to secede from the United
States. Bettie wrote, "Well the election day has at last arrived. I think the
ordinance of secession will be voted for by a great majority of the
people. We made a flag this evening for Wesley. We are going to see the
cavalry pass next week." She also made her brother David a flag the day
before as she noted "The fight has begun. A Federal vessel at Norfolk
was shot all to pieces."

Life during the agitated states of affairs was somewhat normal at
the Graham Mansion. Bettie sewed, ordered silks from Richmond,
bought calico dresses at the store at the "Forge." She read much and
noted it in her journal from the varied works of Arctic Explorations of
Dr. Kane, Blair's Lecture on Taste, to Alexander Pope's translation of
The Iliad. While her sister Mary joined the church, Bettie turned down
"Mr. Miles" attempts to get her to join stating, "I told him that he
wouldn't want such a bad thing as I in the church." Her journal writing
became less frequent. She missed over a month from June 13 until July
29 during which time the battle of First Manassas or First Bull Run
occurred. The Yankees preferred to name battles for nearby natural

landmarks such as streams, where as Southerners named battles for nearby towns or cities.

On September 8, 1861, James G. Tate wrote his sister Nannie from Fairfax County in Northern Virginia expressing the early feelings of excitement that young men feel in war that slowly erode when the bleak reality hits them. "It is now pouring down rain. This is one of the many pleasures of a soldier's life. Who wouldn't be a soldier!"

Back in the almost forgotten theater of war over the mountains in present day West Virginia, the 51st joined the 3rd Brigade in the Army of the Kanawha, taking part in Sewell Mountain Campaign. Robert E. Lee arrived on September 21 to take command. Rufus Woolwine and John T. Washburn heard Reverend G. S. Tuggle preach and they slept in the pulpit the same night. Woolwine celebrated his birthday on October 20 at Raleigh Court House noting, "I enjoy our social activities, the association with ladies and gentlemen of like background, and the many warm friendships that have resulted, both locally, and all over the south."

Lee failed to meet his chief objective: preventing the Union forces from organizing these western counties into a new state. The Confederates lost control of the Kanawha Valley and retreated into the mountains. Disease, terrible weather, impassable roads, and lack of supplies including weapons, food, and shelter caused terrible hardships for the new troops resulting in death and desertion.

Back at the Graham Mansion in October, Bettie noted her mother's continuing erratic behavior. On the 9th, "Ma has been cutting up terribly this morning, saying we would disgrace ourselves." The next day she noted, "I promised Willie I wouldn't smoke anymore, so I have given all my segars away to Bell Peirce. I have quit whistling also, under promise to the same personage."

The men learned the hard lessons of war quickly. During their initial training, the troops received three days' rations. They ate all the rations at once and went hungry for two days. During the first year of the war, Woolwine "messed" or ate with N. C. Akers, J. F. Via, his brother D. G. Via, J. J. Vaughn, Tiller Thomas, and William Dennis Via until the reorganization of the regiment in 1862.

Woolwine traveled home to Patrick for one of his many visits during the war. On his return, the 51st transferred to take part in the defense of Fort Donelson, Tennessee, in 1862. The regiment traveled to Bowling Green, Kentucky to assist General Albert Sidney Johnston in his unsuccessful attempt to stop General Ulysses S. Grant. General John B. Floyd, a former governor of Virginia, commanded a division including the 51st.

The trip to the "Bluegrass State" took eight days for the regiment. The men traveled via five railroads to Bristol, Knoxville, Chattanooga, Nashville, and Bowling Green. During the stay in Kentucky, Woolwine reported the death of General Felix Zollicoffer at the Battle of Mill Springs on January 17, 1862, and his first pay: "Here we drawed the first money we ever drawed from the time we come into the service." James I. Robertson quotes General Floyd on the 51st in 1862 saying, "They have not a single dollar to purchase the least little comfort, even for the sick."

U. S. Grant earned the moniker "Unconditional Surrender" when he forced the capitulation of Fort Henry and Fort Donelson. The 51st Virginia under the command of another VMI graduate, Colonel James W. Massie, fought in the thick at Fort Donelson in February 1862. This battle was a rugged baptism into the rigors of war for the young Patrick Countians.

Rufus Woolwine wrote of the battle, "There we took a boat for Fort Donelson. Got there that night. On Wednesday the Twelfth of February we was marched out for fight. Worked all night throwing up breastworks. On the thirteenth, we lay in our ditches all day and such heavy cannonading was never heard before. That night it rained and we just had to lay in our ditches. Fourteenth, skirmishing along the line. Lay in our ditches that night. Fifteenth, just as day began to dawn upon the silvery waters of the Cumberland we engaged the enemy and drove him from his camp. When we succeeded in ascending the first hill such a sight my eyes never before beheld. Twas there I beheld the mangled dead and dying, laying in all imaginable forms. Yes, there several hundred miles from our native homes, and from those that was bound to us by the strongest ties of affection. I am happy to say that thanks to God Virginians done their duty as becomes true men and patriots. Though distantly situated, they thought of their happy homes far away that they was fighting for. With them as with all of Jeff's boys, they done all men could do."

On February 15, Wharton's Brigade attacked the Federal right and opened an escape route at the cost of 9 killed, 43 wounded and 5 missing. The sniping generals, Floyd and Pillow, failed to follow up the success of the breakout. The next day Floyd's command escaped before the surrender of the fort. The men made their way to Nashville, Chattanooga, and finally to Abingdon. Going into winter camp at Glade Spring, the wounded recuperated in the hospital at Emory and Henry College.

The 51st continued in Wharton's Brigade in the Army of the Kanawha and remained in the Department of Southwestern Virginia through the rest of 1862. Captain David Lee Ross resigned from the company and returned to his farm at Elamsville. He assumed command of the county militia with the title of Lieutenant Colonel. Later in the war, authorities inducted all militiamen into service. Ross then joined the 21st Virginia Cavalry Regiment.

Wharton's brigade returned to Virginia in the spring of 1862 and occupied the Kanawha Valley the following September. Though a promotion for Wharton was in order, he still remained a colonel. His slow promotions throughout the war resulted from a stormy relationship with Jefferson Davis.

On Monday, February 17, 1862, Bettie Graham wrote, "There is a reported fight at Fort Donnelson." The next day she wrote, "Fort Donnelson has been surrendered." Followed the next day by "Jay came from town this evening. He brought a dispatch from Brother saying he was safe. Oh! how much relieved we were to hear of it." On Saturday, February 22, George Washington's birthday, the Confederate States of America inaugurated Jefferson F. Davis as their one and only President. Bettie noted, "The rain has been pouring in torrents all day, a bad day for the inauguration of our first President." She noted the day before "Mr. Robinson stopped on his way to North Carolina to hire negroes. Made some preserves (apple), also some yeast. Heard this evening that there was fighting going on at Nashville, and that General (Albert Sidney) Johnston had telegraphed to our Generals to surrender the city, but I don't believe one word of it."

August Forsberg commented in his diary about the service of Major Graham. "The morning of the 10th (March 1862) I was lifted on my horse, and followed my regiment as long as I could do so mounted. Two o'clock P. M. was agreed upon by the Commanders for the attack in front & rear, but our guide had taken us by such a route that when Gen. Williams commenced firing, we were yet some miles from the position assigned us. At the first report of the guns in front of town we were ordered to 'double quick'. In the excitement I forgot all about the pain in my wounded knee, dismounted and with aid of my sword, used as a walking cane, I hobbled along with my men. The weather was intensely hot and the men, being moved so rapidly over such rough ground, soon became exhausted and scattered. I reached the position in rear of town, with only a handful of men, just as a Federal wagon train was making its way out. It was fired into and forced to return. The enemy, observing his communications with the rear threatened, advanced most of his available Infantry to dislodge us from the ridge we occupied, and, assisted by a battery within easy range, he was not far from success. But for the stubborn defence made principally by Capt. Graham of the 51st and his company nearest to the road, the day may not have been ours. Until dark firing continued on both sides, without any advantage gained. Daring the night the Feds burned some of their stores, and evacuated the town successfully- I suppose very much to their own surprise. The engagement at Fayette C. H. was heralded as a great triumph to the Southern Army, but the fact that Col. Sieber with his inferior Federal force escaped unmolested during the night with his artillery and most of his trains, proves, I believe, his superior management, or great oversight on our part."

On March 11, David P. Graham came home on furlough from the war. Bettie noted it in her journal. Two weeks later, she noted his stay was extended until May 1. On March 28, she wrote that her brother's horse hurt his arm. She noted on April 6 that they were surprised by "the arrival of Captain Forsberg and Major Densy. They are going to church today." The next day, "The rain has kept the gentlemen with us today." The next day she played "Charity" on the piano for the visitors and "Captain Forsberg paid great attention and thought it very fine." The happy interlude ended on April 11 when the guests left, but they were back eleven days later. One wonders if the officers were interested in the charms of Miss Bettie Graham. It was a long way from Forsberg's Sweden to Wythe County, Virginia. Sensing this brother

David would not allow her to give Forsberg a "needle case." She gave it to him anyway on April 27. On May 1, she noted a year passing since leaving Baltimore, Maryland, on the way home from Philadelphia. Forsberg was not the only man interested in Bettie Graham. Two days later she wrote, "Went to the Forge. I rode Wesley's horse and the girt broke and I fell off. Mr. Robinson came back with me in the buggy." Mr. Robinson was either her future father-in-law or future husband John Robinson, who was a partner with her brother David in business.

At the beginning of the war, soldiers elected their own officers. When the 51st reorganized in 1862, William Tyler Akers became captain of Company D. Woolwine received promotion to Second Lieutenant. He went to work as adjutant, purchasing supplies and salt, and recruiting in the counties of Scott, Tazewell and Patrick. Special duties including that of recruitment brought him home to Patrick County many times. During one of these visits, he arrested two "bushwhackers." Other duties included arresting men for making and selling liquor in Giles County in July 1862. He visited Patrick County in 1862 on May 5 through May 25, November 21 through December 12, and December 21 through the 28.

Bettie Graham continued to write about the home front in Wythe County visiting her brother David in Wytheville during May. "We were in Brother's tent and had refreshments consisting of dried huckleberries."

She noted her brother was suffering with a boil on his back. She noted that there was some "beau hunting" going on writing, "As we were coming out of church some of the men who belonged to Otey's battery said 'I wish some of these young ladies would ask me to go home with them.' We went on however without catching a beau until we got back to the bank, where were stationed Col. Wharton, Capt. Forsberg, Major Denessy and Lt. Tate. I walked on with the Capt. Nan came next with the Col. Mary with the Major and Lid with the Lieut. They staid until twelve o'clock. At night Mary A. took off her shoes and found her feet all swollen. We raised a great laugh on her about it, telling her that her feet swelled with the effort to catch a beau, and that she ran her feet off running after the beaux, etc."

She mentioned her future sister-in-law, Nannie Tate writing on May 13, "Nannie and I had a tooth pulled. She screamed, but I did not." Death came from now battlefield sources noting the death of Emily Watson on June 8, 1862. Bettie's journal's last entry was on June 21.

In June 1862, William Hanson Tate wrote of the man who one day in the future would marry his sister, Nannie. "Captain Graham arrived late Saturday evening. We were much rejoiced to meet him. He is not looking well." David Peirce Graham like many men serving in the war experienced health problems caused by exposure to new diseases or the stress of the war and the responsibility of taking men into battles where the loss of life was extremely prevalent.

One of the principal objectives of the Union forces involved capturing the salt mines at Saltville and the lead mines in Wythe County. These threats required the Confederate government to keep forces in southwest Virginia to protect these sources. The mines were essential to the Confederate armies as the largest sources of both salt and lead were in southwest Virginia. In the spring of 1862, the 51st went to meet a Federal force that had captured Princeton, Virginia, now West Virginia. The regiment succeeded in driving the Federal forces from the nearly destroyed town.

A unit of the 51st under Captain William T. Akers traveled to White Sulphur Springs and lost to a stronger Federal force. Captain Akers and his troops escaped by burning a bridge behind them. In June 1862, the 51st returned to Giles County. Later that month, it encamped at Peterstown, now in West Virginia. On July 3, the unit assisted in defeating a Federal force at Mercer Courthouse. For the next several weeks, members of the 51st remained in camp near Narrows in Giles County.

In August 1862, General W. W. Loring assumed command of the Department of Southwestern Virginia. Wharton's Brigade (including the 51st and 50th Regiments and 23rd Battalion of Infantry along with Stamp's Artillery) moved into Monroe County and at Lewisburg on August 28 routed a Federal force led by future president Colonel Rutherford B. Hayes.

Threatened by a much larger Union army, Wharton returned to Narrows. The 51st Regiment, now under command of Lieutenant Colonel Augustus Forsberg, moved to Grey Sulphur Springs where it drilled for several weeks and served on picket duty. In early September 1862, the brigade moved back into present day West Virginia and defeated a Federal force at Montgomery Ferry on the Kanawha River. It captured a large quantity of supplies including food, clothing, and arms.

The Confederates again occupied Charleston, driving the Federal forces toward the Ohio River. They camped for several weeks, enjoying the luxury of the captured supplies. Loring decided to move from Charleston back to the Greenbrier River. General Lee replaced him with General John Echols and ordered the unit back to Charleston, but a large Federal army already occupied the city. The brigade returned to Narrows, Virginia, where it remained for the winter of 1862-1863.

Rufus James Woolwine of the 51st Virginia Infantry of Patrick County,
Virginia, kept a journal of his wartime experiences.
(Courtesy of the Virginia Historical Society.)

Chapter Four
The War of Secession

In the theater of war involving the Union Army of the Potomac and Robert E. Lee's Army of Northern Virginia mainly between Richmond, Virginia, and Washington, D. C., battles occurred around Richmond in June and July 1862 known as the Seven Days. The armies returned back to Second Manassas and to the banks of a Maryland stream called Antietam for a fight that Southerners called Sharpsburg. After returning to Virginia, Lee held off the Yankees of the banks of the Rappahannock River at Fredericksburg on December 13.

On December 21, 1862 from Port Royal Virginia in Caroline County with "Stonewall" Jackson, James G. Tate wrote his sister about a recent encounter with Union forces. "We did not get to fire. We were fired upon." Eleven days later President Abraham Lincoln released the Emancipation Proclamation freeing all slaves in parts of the country in "rebellion against the United States" and thereby freeing the slaves belonging to the Grahams. Although this was paper freedom that did not take effect until the end of the war. This action kept the European powers such as England and France from coming into the war on the side of the South.

As 1862 became 1863, James G. Tate wrote his father, Charles C. Tate, from Caroline County outside Fredericksburg about a recent exploit of J. E. B. Stuart at Kelly's Ford in Culpeper County upstream on the Rappahannock River. "No doubt you saw an account of Stuart's fight with the enemy. It was a right brilliant little affair." Tate, though experiencing the hardships of war, specifically the lack of consistent food wrote, "We were about as glad to see the baker and skillet as anything."

In March 1863, Colonel Wharton received orders from General Samuel Jones, commanding the Department of Western Virginia, to place his brigade where it could defend the lead mines, the salt wells, and the Virginia and Tennessee Railroad in southwest Virginia. He established headquarters at Glade Springs, Virginia. His command of 1,154 men included the 51st and 50th Virginia Regiments, the 30th Virginia Battalion of Infantry, and Stamp's Artillery.

Desertions became a serious problem and the recruitment of replacements became necessary. Lieutenant Woolwine headed a recruitment team that had some success getting sixteen men and found those making and selling whiskey and returned six deserters from Company A in Russell and Wise counties.

In June 1863, the 51st moved into Tennessee to support General

Buckner's forces near Chattanooga where an expected attack did not appear. After two weeks, the regiment returned to Glade Springs. On June 27, Confederate cavalry drove away a Federal force at Saltville. Colonel Wharton reported that the 51st had 972 men.

After taking the train to Staunton, the troops marched to Woodstock and joined the Army of Northern Virginia under General Robert E. Lee on his march away from Gettysburg. On July 8, Wharton received promotion to Brigadier General and Forsberg to Colonel of the 51st.

David Peirce Graham was at the White Sulphur Springs in present day West Virginia in February 1863 acting as Commandant of the Post. He received promotion to Major on July 8, 1863, thus becoming Major David Graham and giving his home in Wythe County the name most know it, by Major Graham's Mansion.

Early in August, General Lee ordered Wharton's Brigade to Warm Springs to block Federal General Averell's advance. Averell backed off and returned to West Virginia. During the summer of 1863, the 51st marched from Staunton to Glade Springs via Winchester, Orange Courthouse, Warm Springs, Dublin Depot, Abingdon, and Jonesboro, Tennessee.

Near the end of August, the brigade returned to southwest

Virginia as the Federals made a determined effort to destroy the salt works, the lead mines, and the railroad. They captured Bristol and burned the town. The Confederates gathered all the forces they could get to oppose the Federals. At the last minute, the Union forces under General Burnside gave up the effort and returned to Knoxville. The Confederates pursued as far as Jonesboro, Tennessee.

General Robert Ransom assumed command of the Department of Western Virginia and Eastern Tennessee. He moved Wharton's Brigade to Blountville, Tennessee, to support General Longstreet who was trying to recapture Knoxville. All during the autumn of 1863, the 51st marched and counter-marched in the Rogersville-Bean Station area of Tennessee between the Holston River and the Clinch Mountains, expecting contact with the enemy at all times but seeing little fighting.

Across the Commonwealth of Virginia James G. Tate experienced war first hand with the loss of commanding General Thomas J. "Stonewall" Jackson on May 10, 1863, after the Battle of Chancellorsville. Lee moved his army into Pennsylvania and the three day battle of Gettysburg. After returning to Virginia, the "Winter of Discontent" set in on the army. James wrote to his father on October 13, 1863, "We have crossed four streams since leaving Orange County. We had to wade the first three and it was most too cool to be very pleasant."

After the disastrous Battle of Bristow Station, Tate wrote a week later, "I don't deem it necessary to give you any particulars of what has been done as I presume the papers have kept you posted. We have done some right hard marching and have had some very bad weather for it. The whole affair turned out pretty much as I expected it would from the signs of the time. There was no general engagement. It seems General Lee not being able to cut Meade off didn't care to engage him at all." George Gordon Meade, the commander of the Union Army of the Potomac, sparred with Robert E. Lee across Northern Virginia in the winter of 1863-64 before the two armies went into winter quarters with Lee and his army south of the Rappahannock River in Orange County, Virginia, and Meade in Culpeper north of the river.

On January 9, 1864, James wrote Nannie from Pisgah Church in Orange County, "You wished to know how I spent my Xmas. I had quite a quiet time I do assure you. Oh, I would have been so glad to have been able to spend it with you. I fear it will be a long time yet ere I am permitted to enjoy that pleasure."

In January 1864, the 51st marched in General Longstreet's failed attempt to trap a Federal force near Dandridge, Tennessee. Many of the men had no shoes, and their bleeding feet left red marks in the snow. The men spent much time foraging during the bitterly cold winter, for in addition to food, they lacked good clothing and shelter. The harsh winter took the lives of a number of soldiers. In one month, the strength of Wharton's Brigade (including the 51st and 45th Regiments and 30th Battalion of Infantry) dropped from 915 to 725 men.

The brigade, barely at the strength of a regiment, moved to Bull's Gap to protect the headquarters of the Department of East Tennessee in February. They repaired roads and performed picket duty. They had not seen battle in over a year.

Woolwine witnessed the execution of deserters in Tennessee. By February, he was back in Patrick County attending a "Frollick at Widow Celah Hubbard." He continued a myriad of duties from commanding the company in April to acting as adjutant to Lieutenant Colonel John Wolfe.

In April 1864, the regiment marched to Abingdon in terrible weather over the muddiest possible roads. Woolwine presided over the execution of a deserter, writing, "the regiment being formed in two battalions to march out to the execution of John H. Jones of 30th Battalion Sharp Shooters of Grayson County for desertion. He was executed at two o'clock p.m."

On April 23, 1864, Major David Peirce Graham resigned his position due to health reasons. His service in the 51st Virginia was not stellar, but he lasted longer than most and like many the war broke his health at least temporarily.

Early in May 1864, General Lee reorganized the Army of Southwest Virginia and placed General John C. Breckinridge, a former vice president of the United States, in charge. The 51st, stationed at Narrows, Virginia, transferred north to the Valley of Virginia on May 6, 1864, riding the train to Staunton and marching north, down the valley, to meet the oncoming Federals. Wharton pushed the brigade of 1557 men (including 30th Virginia Infantry, the 62nd Mounted Infantry, and Company A of the 1st Missouri Cavalry along with the 51st) an amazing 187 miles in 8 days.

On May 1, William H. Tate wrote to his sister, Nannie, the future Mrs. David P. Graham, from his camp near Dublin in Pulaski County, Virginia. He expressed inner conflict about wanting to come visit, but duty was stronger. He wrote, "bad example to the men who are rather predisposed to such things...You have no idea what a conflict has been going on between my inclinations and my duty, but under the present circumstances I believe it to be my duty to remain with the company." The desire for simple survival continued to be a theme for Tate and others. He wrote, "If you an opportunity I want you to send me something to eat."

On May 13, Wharton's Brigade as part of Breckinridge's

Division in the Army of Northern Virginia halted two miles south of New Market. The cadets from Virginia Military Institute joined the brigade there. At the famous Battle of New Market, the 51st was on the front line in the thick of the fight under command of Lieutenant Colonel John P. Wolfe using the Keydets as reserves to drive the Federals from the field.

On May 15, Woolwine wrote, "at one o'clock company moved out for New Market in the county of Shenandoah. Day very inclement. Threw up rail works some two or three miles from New Market. Enemy did not advance. Marched forward and attacked the town at 9 am. Whipped and drove the enemy across the North Fork of the Shenandoah River. They burnt the bridge. We captured many prisoners, five pieces of artillery, wagons, and small arms."

The terrible loss of war hit the Tate family for the first time after New Market on May 15, but with the communications of that day, it was several days before they knew it and it would not be the last time they knew loss. On May 19, 1864, a telegraph from R. C. Graham to Mrs. A. C. Hanson announced sad news from the battlefield of New Market. "Dear Sister, Sad News. William Tate and Charlie Crockett killed. Their remains on the cars and will be up on the first train." William Tate rests today at Fort Chiswell Cemetery in Wythe County.

After New Market, General Lee ordered General Breckinridge's troops to proceed to Hanover County to aid in the defense of Richmond. The entire regiment now numbered 588 men. They defended the junction of the Virginia Central Railroad with the Richmond, Fredericksburg, and Potomac lines. The 51st successfully prevented the destruction of the bridge over the South Anna River and repelled a Federal attack near Henry Clay's birthplace on May 28. Companies A and D, led by Major William T. Akers, skirmished with Federal troops and lost four men.

Fighting continued throughout the area after the Battle of the Wilderness as General Grant engaged in his relentless campaign to wear down Lee's troops and capture Richmond. In the battles of Mechanicsville, Cold Harbor, and Frayser's Farm, the 51st suffered heavy losses.

Woolwine reported they took a train, the "General Stuart," and went to Hanover Junction. The 51st joined the Army of Northern Virginia. Woolwine wrote, "heavy skirmishing along the entire. Enemy moved last night. Great many troops coming in. Saw General R. E. Lee...Passed Ashland and camped near where Henry Clay was born." A few days later he writes," Twenty ninth, Fortified. Thirtieth, some skirmishing...Thirty-first, Had to fall back under a galling fire. Joseph Rose killed. Heavy firing from artillery. During the day sharpshooters kept very busy. June first, drove them from their rifle pits...That night we were relieved and marched to Mechanicsville. Slept a few hours and day dawned. Second, To Chickahominy. At Gaines Farm drove their sharpshooters from their pits and fortified. Third, at dawn of day enemy attacked General Echols. They were handsomely repulsed with great slaughter to them." This battle took its name from a local tavern named Cold Harbor.

On June 7, General Lee ordered Breckinridge's forces back to the Shenandoah Valley to block the advance of the Federals under General David Hunter. Born in the Shenandoah Valley, Hunter, a militant abolitionist, seemed to relish punishing the Southerners. He burned much of Staunton and Buchanan, captured Lexington, and burned the Virginia Military Institute along with most of the town. His forces captured Liberty, now Bedford, and fully expected to capture Lynchburg, which served as the junction of the railroads on which the Southerners depended on for arms and food; its capture would have been a serious blow to the Confederates.

General Wharton assumed temporary command of the division as Breckinridge recovered from wounds received at Cold Harbor, and the brigade took the train to Lynchburg. By June 16, the 51st built breastworks near Thomas Jefferson's Poplar Forest and, by various ruses such as marching and counter-marching for the next two days, outwitted General Hunter. After severe fighting, Hunter retreated from the city back toward Liberty. Confederate forces followed and engaged Hunter at Hanging Rock near Salem defeating him.

In a period of a month, the 51st assisted in repelling three superior armies at New Market, Cold Harbor, and Lynchburg. On June 16, Woolwine wrote, "Left an hour early and marched for Lynchburg, distant 13 miles. Passed through city to camp west of fair grounds. I went back to town and had quite a nice time."

The 51st, now a part of Franklin County native Jubal Early's command, serving in Wharton's Brigade, Echols' Division, chased Hunter into West Virginia. The regiment fought for Early in the Shenandoah Valley Campaign of 1864. They marched almost constantly for three months and Woolwine rose in rank from first lieutenant to captain.

Late in June 1864, the army started down the Shenandoah Valley and reached Winchester in early July. It captured large quantities of food and other supplies abandoned by the retreating Federal forces. After a day's rest, plenty of food, and some new clothes, the 51st marched to Martinsburg, Virginia, now West Virginia, where it chased away a Federal force under General Franz Sigel. After crossing the Potomac

River and routing several more Federal forces, it proceeded toward Washington. On July 8, the regiment repelled an attack at Middletown as fighting occurred at the Battle of Monocacy.

Woolwine reports on July 9, 1864, "On to Frederick City. Layed in line of battle all day. Gordon's division whipped the enemy. We crossed Monocosy (Monocacy) River, camped for the night." On the Eleventh, he wrote, "Went within 5 miles of city Washington." Echols Division guarded the trains, and although ordered up it never engaged in the fighting. A few days later Rufus wrote, "Heard sermon from third chapter 18th verse James by Rev Brillheart on the bank of the Opequon." The verse ironically reads, "And the fruit of righteousness is sown in peace of them that make peace."

On July 10, the army camped only five miles from Washington. The regiment remained there two days within sight of the Federal Capitol. General Early thought it too risky due to the large Federal forces on its way to protect the city. He crossed the Potomac into Virginia where he encountered and defeated several small Federal forces. Temporarily, all Federal forces were out of the Shenandoah Valley. Shortly thereafter, General Early's cavalry crossed back over the Potomac and burned the town of Chambersburg, Pennsylvania in retaliation for the burning of Staunton, Lexington, and Buchanan by

General Hunter. The 51st stayed near Sharpsburg, Maryland, while McCausland burned Chambersburg. Early's men returned to Virginia and camped in the Winchester area.

In August 1864, General Philip Sheridan assumed command of the Federal forces and launched an offensive against Early in the Shenandoah Valley. He began a relentless campaign that resulted in the complete destruction of the Valley. In a series of battles, General Early's troops retreated south up the Valley.

Woolwine wrote on August 12, "Left before day. Moved on in direction of Strasburg, passing Middletown. Formed line of Battle on Hupp's Hill near Strasburg. Some skirmishing. Remained all day. At night to Fisher's Hill. Formed our command on right of road. Thirteenth through the seventeenth threw up some works. Some skirmishing. Seventieth, the enemy had gone. Pursued and fought at Winchester. Took the fort. Lost of 51st was 3 killed, 28 wounded. Ladies met us on the field."

On August 22, while Early advanced up to the Maryland line, Woolwine wrote, "stopped our brigade at an old church known as Trinity church, built during the reign of Ann Queen of England. In rear of the crumbling structure and dilapidated walls is a grave with the following inscription: 'Sacred to the memory of John Baker who departed this life

May 30, 1798, aged 67 years.' I went to town and saw the identical spot where justice overtook John Brown." He witnessed the twenty-second execution of a fellow Confederate for desertion.

On August 25 he wrote, "Moved out at sunrise, crossed fields and old road. Struck pike at Leetown. We passed beyond church. Loaded. Sent 51st forward as skirmishers. Engaged the enemy and drove them a piece. Enemy flanked us and we had to fall back. Our loss in killed, wounded and captured was 102. Lt Col Wolfe and Lt John Akers were among the slain." The next day he wrote, "We moved back by the old battleground, passed the usual horrors of war, over Col. (John P.) Wolfe's grave and went to church and camped for the night."

On August 25, 1864, James Graham Tate lost his life at Shepherdstown, Virginia, now West Virginia, after receiving and surviving wounds at Malvern Hill in July 1862 and at Chancellorsville in May 1863. A family letter from a month later summed it up this way. "The death of him whom we all loved so well, my heart bled a fresh for the Father and loved one at home who again have been so sorely bereaved...Yes the WAR still goes on and tho many of the noblest, bravest, best have fallen, the grave unsatisfied, insatiate still cries for more...from every battlefield comes the wail of the wounded and the dying…to heart and…until we cry in anguish of soul How Long, Oh Lord, How Long?"

Picket duty occupied the 51st from September 15 until the nineteenth at Stephenson's Depot near Winchester. Heavy fighting occurred with heavy losses. Members of the 51st scattered several times, and a number fell into enemy hands. During the fighting around Winchester, William Tyler Akers received promotion to major and for a time commanded the 51st Regiment. R. J. Woolwine replaced him as captain of Company D. The Confederates won some skirmishes, but could not hold out against Sheridan's relentless pressure from far superior numbers.

During September, Woolwine and the 51st fought at Fisher's Hill on September 22 with Wharton's Brigade (including the 45th Virginia and the 30th Battalion of Infantry). The regiment was the size of a company and the brigade had only 417 men. Woolwine wrote on the nineteenth, "enemy attacked flanks of Thirtieth Virginia Battalion. We fell back and formed our line nearer town and repulsed them several times ordered to Winchester, then move to rear and repulsed enemy. Our line was giving way, but we fell back in good order to our works. From there we got out in great confusion. Loss heavy. Continued the retreat…sent to Strasburg to stop stragglers. During engagement enemy rode over me and I captured a horse and came out on it. The same was stolen from me at Strasburg. Loss was five kelled fifty five wounded and seventy four captured." On the twenty-second he wrote of the Battle of Fisher's Hill, "I received the order announcing my promotion to the Captaincy of Co D. We stampeded." Three of the 51st died and 28 were wounded.

Reinforcements joined the brigade while it waited for a chance to go on the offensive. On October 13, 1864, the Confederates reentered the Valley and marched toward Winchester where they encountered Sheridan's army at Cedar Creek.

At first, General Early's troops drove back the Federals. The 51st, led by Major W. T. Akers, charged a Federal entrenchment and succeeded in driving the Federals away, but superior strength prevailed and Major Akers' forces fell back. The Union Sixth Corps and cavalry wrecked the 51st. The retreat soon turned into confusion that resulted in a rout. General Early retreated up the Valley to New Market. Woolwine wrote of the Battle of Cedar Creek on October 19, "Moved out at one o'clock a. m. Some of the army flanked. We moved in front and drove enemy out of their camp on the hill at Cedar Creek. But at 4:30 p.m. the tide of battle turned and we fled the field back to Fisher's Hill."

Later that month Woolwine wrote, "Took train for Richmond,

Visited soldier's home and Camp Lee." During November and December he reported, "Snowed and Hailed...On working detail. Had the misfortune to get one man killed. Private Henry Lindsey Co. I, 50th Regiment, Carroll County Va. 45th VA Regiment refused to drill 51st went to arrest those that refused to drill, my Company took possession of their arms...I took command of the 45 Regiment."

The 51st moved to New Market and into winter quarters. On December 16, Wharton's men, the only Confederates left in the Shenandoah Valley, moved to Fishersville in Augusta County. Since June 1864, the 51st had marched 1,670 miles and participated in 75 battles or skirmishes.

In January at Fishersville Woolwine wrote, "Where oh where shall I be twelve months hence? Perhaps in vast eternity. All are now taking their sweet repose. Lt. Cheely and myself are enjoying ourselves eating fine apples. Have just completed my pay rolls." He returned to Patrick County for almost a month in January and February 1865 continuing to attend "Frollicks." His uncle, Notley P. Adams, sent General Early $250 in Confederate money.

The Battle of Waynesboro on March 2, 1865 began with sleet and snow falling as the regiment prepared to cross the North Fork of the Shenandoah River. Wharton reported that his division (including the

45th, 50th, and 51st Virginia Regiments and 30th Battalion Virginia Infantry) had 800 men against 7500 "splendidly equipped" Federal cavalry under the immediate command of George Custer and overall command of Phillip Sheridan. Colonel Forsberg commanded the brigade with Major Akers commanding the 51st on its last battlefield. The cavalry surrounded them, and most of the regiment surrendered. Woolwine wrote, "There we was all captured."

Rufus Woolwine's career as a soldier for the Confederate States of America was over. He served from the very beginning in 1861 and fought to within one month of the end. He saw twenty-two men executed for desertion. His duties included recruiting, chasing deserters, catching whiskey makers, acting as messenger, and fighting beside his men as an infantryman.

General Wharton and the rest of the 51st Virginia joined the Army of Northern Virginia and served under General John B. Gordon. Forces of the United States captured most of those left along with their battle flag on March 25 at Fort Stedman. Wharton went to Lynchburg to defend the city and was at Christiansburg on April 10 when he heard of Lee's surrender. The 51st Virginia Infantry Regiment disbanded that day.

After the war, Wharton lived and married in Radford, Virginia. He served two terms in the Virginia Senate, where he was involved in the creation of Virginia Tech. When he died in 1906, his family wrapped him in the battle flag of the 51st Virginia Infantry Regiment.

The prisoners from Waynesboro marched to Staunton, Winchester, and Harper's Ferry and then to prisons at Elmira, New York and Fort Delaware. Captain Woolwine and most of his company went to Fort Delaware. On March 9, he wrote of leaving Harper's Ferry, traveling to Baltimore and staying in prison at Fort McHenry, the site of Francis Scott Key's immortal poem that is today our national anthem.

Fort Delaware, completed in 1859 after ten years of construction, is today a state park on Pea Patch Island in the Delaware River outside present day Wilmington. The river is ten miles wide at the site half way between New Jersey and Delaware. Brigadier General Alban F. Schoepf commanded the prison when the members of the 51st Virginia Infantry arrived on March 11, 1865. Schoepf, born in Poland in 1822 and educated in Vienna, served in the Austrian army until he joined a failed Hungarian revolt. He escaped to Syria and made his way to North America in 1851. After working in the U. S. Patent Office and War Department, he fought early in the war in Kentucky.

Prison life at Fort Delaware involved living in a T-shaped barracks divided for officers and enlisted men. Described as lice-infested in the summer and bitterly cold in the winter, the quarters consisted of bunks stacked four high. Food for a day consisted of, "one small loaf of bread and one small piece of meat, together with a half pint or sometimes a pint of weak vegetable juice soup." The following is a stanza of a song rendered by the prisoners at Fort Delaware.

> "Now white folks here's a moral; dars nothing true below
> For life is but a tater patch, the debil has to hoe
> Ebery one has his troubles here, tho's he go near and far,
> But the most unlucky debil, is the prisoner of war."

During Woolwine's imprisonment, he continued writing: "March 24th, drawn one pair of drawers. 25th, drawn one pair socks. April third, Drawn one blanket, 1 pair drawers, heard of the fall of Richmond. Fourth salute fired." On the twentieth he wrote, "Where will Lt (John M.) Cemise and myself be one month hence? At home well and hearty I fondly hope." On the twenty-sixth he wrote, "Oh what a lovely day. How much I wish I was in old Patrick this beautiful evening. At _____ with Miss _____, yes the beautiful accomplished _____. The sole subject of all my earthly affection. Oh what a proud consolation it would be to know that she is well and still thinks of her absent, as well as unchanging friend, Rufus." He read books in prison including The New Testament, The Wild West Scenes, Tempest and Sunshine and volume one of The Conquest of Mexico.

Religion continued to be a strong theme in his writing. On Sunday the 30th he wrote, "Glad would I be to quit the life of a prisoner of war and return to my quiet home in the mountains of Patrick. There to rest from the cares and troubles of a four years hard campaigning. I'll trust a merciful god. Myself and Captain Dobyns expects to be at home to day one month hence." On Sunday, May 14, Woolwine wrote of the Charity meeting, "Oh how much I wish I was there. To mingle with old friends that I love so much. I truly hope to be there at the next meeting." The next day he wrote, "My motto is Trust to Luck. Would like to exchange my present abode for my home in old Patrick. Just had a pleasant nap. I was far far away from here in my dreams." The following Sunday he wrote, "Today is Jack Creek meeting. Wish I was there to mingle with friends and relatives, but alas! I see no prospects of a speedy release from this place. Well! I await patiently the action of the government...From this time forward I shall earnestly endeavor to quit the habit of using tobacco in any way whatever." Sprinkled among his writings were quotes in Latin such as "Whilst I Breathe I Hope" and "Never Despair."

Dr. James A. Davis, President of Shenandoah University, wrote in *51st Virginia Infantry Regiment* that these men came home to "no cheering crowds or clanging bands," but to "broken fences and fields of weeds." They fought the "forgotten war." Seldom were they with Lee and the Army of Northern Virginia, but they were protecting the salt works and railroads of southwestern Virginia. They experienced everything imaginable including death, disease, desertion, harsh weather and fighting without supplies and the full strength of manpower. In battle, they cleared an escape route from Fort Donelson, saw victory at New Market and marched to within five miles of Washington D. C. with Jubal Early. These men did not fail in their cause because of a lack of courage or skill as fighters. Those who survived moved on with the remainder of their lives.

Woolwine took the Oath of Allegiance on June 17, 1865, and began his return to Patrick County two days later on the steamer "Richard Willing." He arrived home on the June 27 after a trip that took him from Baltimore via water to Newport News and Richmond, where he saw Washington's statue on the Capitol grounds "draped in mourning." As he traveled by railroad toward Lynchburg, he had to get off at Burke's Station and walk, then catch another train to Farmville. He rode the last five miles to Lynchburg on the James River and Kanawha Canal, then caught a train to Elliston and walked home from there. Woolwine ended his journal with these thoughts: "Thus ends a journey of four years through the most eventful campaign known in the history of men or nations. Now that peace once more smiles upon our land and country, let us look to the wise disposer of all human events and implore

Him in His infinite wisdom and mercy to smile upon and bless us, a subjugated people. God grant that our course may be such as to meet with the hearty approval of those in authority, both on earth and in heaven. Oh! That we may yield placid obedience to the laws of our land and the laws of god, so that we may again place our dear old state in her original high standing. And when we shall have done this and have finished our pilgrimage here below, may we all join that celestial host of angels in bright glory to sing praises forever more, to the great Jehovah."

Woolwine settled on Russell Creek in Patrick County, where he manufactured tobacco and sold dry goods. In 1866, he became deputy sheriff of Patrick County. He married Sarah R. Brown in 1868. She received attention from R. J. Reynolds, but chose Woolwine because he had visited her in college. They had four children: Sallie, who married M. V. Stedman; Ada, who married H. S. McKinley; Mabel, who married J. C. Barksdale; and Rufus E. Woolwine, who served as commonwealth attorney of Patrick County for twenty years.

Former Captain Woolwine moved to Stuart, Virginia, and served as sheriff from 1891 until 1904. He lived in retirement until his death on December 4, 1908. The old soldier rests today in the Stuart cemetery near his messmate William Dennis Via. For thirty years, Woolwine served as secretary of the Sunday school at Stuart Methodist Church, where his favorite hymn was "A Charge To Keep I Have." Rufus James Woolwine lived as a good citizen, obeying and even enforcing the laws. He put the war behind him, but left his thoughts and feelings to give us insight into an important time in our history.

On December 6, 1900, an aging man from Sweden rose to speak to the Garland Rodes Camp of the United Confederate Veterans in Lynchburg. Augustus Forsberg said, "Many years have passed since the events I have just narrated, and, like similar details of warfare, not of such importance as to merit a place in history, they will soon be forgotten. But the participants in the struggle of those 'days that tried men's souls' cannot readily forget the trials and perils to which they were exposed."

In July 1913, President Woodrow Wilson presided over the fiftieth anniversary of the Battle of Gettysburg. As a young boy, Wilson, a native Virginian, saw Jefferson Davis brought through Augusta, Georgia, after the Confederate President's capture. This memory was still strong when Wilson spoke at this historic moment saying, "We are made by these tragic, epic things to know what it costs to make a nation—the blood and sacrifice of multitudes of unknown men lifted to a great stature in the view of all generations by knowing no limit to their manly willingness to serve." One veteran from the North and the South represented each side on the platform near Wilson. In a symbolic gesture of reunification, the President grasped the hand of both men simultaneously. Photographs show Dr. William Dennis Via of Patrick County, the Southern soldier holding a Second National Flag of the Confederacy that is on display in the Patrick County Historical Museum.

Born on September 8, 1838, Via enlisted in the Ross Company of the 51st Virginia Infantry in June 1861 serving with Rufus Woolwine. After the war, he married Minnie Via and had five children: Daisy, James, Marcie, Mary, and Posie. Dr. Via, a dentist, served as one of the first Trustees of the town of Stuart and possibly mayor in 1884. Less than a year before his own death, the old soldier still attended reunions, the last one in Jacksonville, Florida. As the last survivor of his mess, his time as Corporal, Company D, 51st Virginia Infantry dominated his thoughts. Dr. Via died on March 6, 1915, and lies today in Stuart town Cemetery near his friend, Rufus James Woolwine. Below is President Thomas Woodrow Wilson and William Dennis Via of Patrick County and the 51st Virginia Infantry at the Gettysburg Reunion in 1913.

On February 20, 1914, reflecting upon the death of his friend Via

wrote the following poem and sent it to Woolwine's daughter.

"Oh! Death thou has taken him away,
  And his suffering was so great.
I stayed with him all I could,
  For he was my last 'messmate'!
My 'mess' have all left me now,
  And I am left here alone.
Captain Woolwine, the last to leave me,
  Our friendship was truly known!
We traveled over mountains and valleys,
  Where crystal streams ran down.
Now all their travelings are over,
  Not one of them can be found!
The Lord has done right with them
  I hope they are all at rest.
Though I am left here alone,
  I hope they are with the blest!
If they are with their Saviour,
  Though I cannot long here remain.
My 'mess' has gone and left me,
  Though true happiness I hope to gain!
We loved and respected each other,
  While we together roamed.
But they have all left me now,
  And I will seek a heavenly home!
Now I hope to meet them all,
  In the sweet bye and bye.
And walk the golden streets of heaven,
  Where we will never, never die!"

Actions of the 51st Virginia Infantry

Army of the Kanawha (Aug.-Dec. 1861)
Gauley River (Sept. 10, 1861)
Carnifax Ferry (Sept. 11, 1861)
Buffalo Mountain (Dec. 13, 1861)
Floyd's Division, Central Army of Kentucky, Dept. #2 (Jan.-Feb. 1862)
Wharton's Brigade, Floyd's Division, Central Army of Kentucky, Dept.#2 (Feb. 1862)
Wharton's Brigade, Floyd's Division, Fort Donelson, Dept. #2 Feb. 1862)
Fort Donelson (Feb. 12-16, 1862)
Wharton's Brigade, Army of the Kanawha (Feb.-May 1862)
Lewisburg and Clarksville (Feb. 18, 1862)
Wharton's Brigade, Army of the Kanawha, Dept. of Southwestern Virginia (May-Sep. 1862)
Mercer and Princeton (May 17-18, 1862)
Lewisburg (Aug. 28, 1862)
Kanawha Campaign (Sept. 1862)
Fayetteville (Sept. 10, 1862)
Charleston (WV) (Sept. 25, 1862)
Wharton's Brigade, Dept. of Western Virginia (Feb.-Oct 1863)
Pikeville, KY (Apr. 15, 1863)
Hanover, VA (Jul. 1, 1863)
Wharton's Brigade, Ransom's Division, Dept. of Western Virginia and East Tennessee (Oct.-Nov. 1863)
Chattanooga Siege (Sept.-Nov. 1863)
Wharton's Brigade, Ransom's Division, Dept. of East Tennessee (Nov. 1863 - Mar. 1864)
Knoxville Siege (Nov.-Dec. 1863)
Wharton's Brigade, Dept. of Western Virginia (Mar.-May 1864)
Wharton's Brigade, Breckinridge's Division, Army of Northern Virginia (May-Jun. 1864)
New Market (May 15, 1864)
North Anna, Hanover Junction (May 22-26, 1864)
Totopotomoy Creek (May 30, 1864)
Wharton's-Forsberg's Brigade, Breckinridge's-Wharton's Division, Valley District, Dept. of Northern Virginia (Jun. 1864 - Mar. 1865)
Cold Harbor (Jun. 1-3, 1864)
Lynchburg Campaign (Jun. 1864)
Frederick, MD (Jul. 7-8, 1864)

Monocacy (Jul. 9, 1864)
Fort Stevens (Washington, D.C.) (Jul. 11, 1864)
Rockville, MD (Jul. 13, 1864)
Kernstown (Jul. 24, 1864)
Winchester (Aug. 17, 1864)
3rd Winchester (Sept. 19, 1864)
Fisher's Hill (Sept. 22, 1864)
Harrisonburg (Sept. 23,1864)
Brown's Gap (Sept. 26, 1864)
Cedar Creek (Oct. 19, 1864)
Leetown, WV (Dec. 1, 1864)
Fisherville (Jan. 7, 1865)
Waynesboro (Mar. 2, 1865)
Ivory Creek (Mar. 3, 1865)
Charlottesville (Mar. 6, 1865)
Fort Stedman (detachment) (Mar. 25, 1865)
Union Furnace (detachment) (Mar. 27, 1865)

Regimental Flag of the 51st Virginia Infantry

August Forsberg of the 51st Virginia Infantry Regiment.

Major David Peirce Graham

Chapter Five
Major David Peirce Graham

Born in 1838, David Peirce Graham lived his entire life along the banks of Cedar Run except for serving in the Civil War, where he became Major David Graham. He inherited and operated the Graham businesses including a store at Graham's Forge along with sister Bettie's husband, John Robinson, after his father, Squire David Graham's death on October 16, 1870.

The Grahams continued to develop their iron business including supplying pig iron to the war effort. One source states he sent "gun metal of the highest quality" to Tredegar Iron Works in Richmond, Virginia, during the war.

In 1868, Major Graham married Nancy "Nannie" Montgomery Tate. They were both descendants of Robert Graham. Robert was Major Graham's grandfather from his second marriage and Nancy's great-grandfather from Robert's first marriage.

The couple had eight children. In descending order they were Elizabeth "Lizzie," who married Edwin Hanson Sanders, David, William Tate, who became a doctor, Martha "Patsy" Peirce, who married William Dixon Sanders, Charles Tate, Katherine "Friel," who married Judge Fulton, James Montgomery, and Robert Calvin Graham.

Major David Graham continued expanding on his home including additions in 1870 and twenty years later in 1890. These additions included a hip-on-hip slate roof with a tower and two dormers with the intention of adding another story that was never built. Included in these were two bow windows and connecting porches along with a bathroom leading one source to say that this home was "surprising and unexpected for this area of Virginia."

By 1881, Graham operated only one iron forge in Wythe County. The post war economy and improvements in Northern technology made the Virginia iron operations such as Graham's obsolete.

Major David Graham inherited 1/3 interest in his father's iron operations and his sisters split 2/3 between them. His sisters married and had children of their own expanding the Graham family.

Mary Bell Graham (1843-1900) married Harold J. Mathews on April 23, 1868. They had four children: Fred, Maria, Elizabeth and Mary.

Elizabeth Anne Graham (1845-1921), who kept the journal during the Civil War, married John W. Robinson (1837-1906) on November 21, 1867. Robinson was David P. Graham's partner in business at Graham's Forge operating a store, a grist mill, and other businesses. Elizabeth and John Robinson had eight children: Graham, Malcolm, Harry, Ernest, John, Julia, Mary Bell and Elizabeth.

John Robinson, born in Bedford, Virginia, was the son of Eldridge H. Robinson and Elizabeth Moorman. He moved to Dublin in Pulaski County before the war and worked in the railroad depot as a clerk. He worked in Giles County after that meeting M. B. Tate, who recruited him to Graham's Forge as an employee for Squire David Graham and son. There in the general store he first met his future wife Elizabeth Anne "Bettie" Graham.

When war broke out Robinson joined his future brother-in-law in Company B of the 51st Virginia Infantry. He served as a lieutenant for a year before returning to Graham's Forge to "superintend the manufacture of iron for use by the Confederate government" considered a vital wartime industry.

As stated he married Bettie Graham on November 21, 1867, and after his father-in-law's death in 1870, he joined his brother-in-law David at Graham's Forge as Graham and Robinson.

After the war, Robinson expanded his business interests with the firm of Gwyn, Oglesby and Co. in Max Meadows, Wythe County in 1866. Two years later, he started Robinson and Co. in Lynchburg, which became Robinson, Tate and Co.

Major David Peirce Graham

Robinson joined M. B. Tate and James Crockett in 1869 to take control of the Cripple Creek iron fields acquiring 4,000 acres of "mineral land," which included nearly all the charcoal iron furnaces in the area. In 1878, David P. Graham joined them and furnaces went up at Foster Falls and Reed Island. Robinson managed these properties until 1890 and was President for another eight years after that. George L. Carter took over operation as Carter Coal and Iron Company. Robinson, Carter and Graham "consolidated a number of small independent iron businesses into a company and built a large blast furnace in Pulaski." Virginia Iron, Coal and Coke took over the operation. Robinson was a large stockholder in the company until his death in 1906.

Emily Maria Graham (1848-1889) married J. Williamson McGavock on November 21, 1871. The couple had ten children: David, John, Ephraim, James Hampton, Parish, Martha, Abigail Jouet, Margaret, Mary Bell and an unnamed infant.

On November 8, 1898, the Wytheville Virginia Enterprise noted the passing of David Peirce Graham stating: "No death has occurred in Wythe County in years that so saddened the people of the whole country as did that of Major David P. Graham on last Saturday evening. He was loved and honored by all who knew him, and appreciated most by those most intimate with him. He was a high minded, noble gentleman, whose generosity to his friends and to the poor he knew no bounds. He was

always ready to help the needy. He was sixty-one years old, was

educated at the Virginia Military Institute, and was a gallant Confederate

soldier. He entered the army soon after he attained his majority, and had

risen in rank to Major of the Fifty-first Virginia Regiment when the war

closed. He was the only son of the late Mr. David Graham, and was

associated with his father in the iron reduction business until 1870 when

death removed the elder member of the firm. After that, he succeeded to

the management of his father's vast and valuable estate, whose wealth at

his death exceeded that of any other man in Southwest Virginia. In 1868

he married Miss Nannie M. Tate, daughter of the late Mr. Charles Tate

and sister of Senator Thomas Tate of Draper's Valley. A short time after

his father's death, he and his brother-in-law, Mr. John W. Robinson,

formed the co-partnership of Graham and Robinson for the purpose of

continuing the iron making business. This firm has continued until the

present, and has conducted many of the largest mining operations in the

Southwest. For the last few years, however Major Graham had given

more attention to his farm, and had lived the comfortable life of a

wealthy and extensive farmer and grazer. Notwithstanding this

preference for the quietude of his farm and for the pleasures of his home,

where he was in constant companionship with his wife and children, his associates in mining enterprises kept him upon the Board of Directors, and other important positions that they might use his splendid executive ability. One of those organizations, the Wythe Lead and Zinc Mines, had re-elected him its president for years. His wealth, integrity, and widely known business capacity gave strength to every company of which he was a member. In his home life he was a devoted husband and father, was kind and indolent to everyone, and was loved as few men are by all who knew him. His wife and eight children survive him, five sons and three daughters. He had been alarmingly ill but a few days, as he went to bed on Monday, and died the following Saturday. His remains were interred in the Graham cemetery near Graham's Forge, in the presence of a large concourse of his sorrowing friends."

Major David P. Graham and his wife, Nannie T. Graham

Census records show the agricultural and personal property of the Grahams from 1860 through 1890. Below are samples of the property at Cedar Run Farm with their values then to the right.

	1860	1870	1880	1890
Horses	32 ($1600)	31($1860)	28($1035)	23($1120)
Cattle	276(3312)	217(5405)	155(4612)	157(3040)
Hogs	285(570)	172(344)	253(812)	75(200)
Carriages	2(400)	11(390)	6(300)	4(300)
Totals	$7,612	6,692	4.350	5,775

David Peirce Graham's life at Cedar Run was very different than his parents. At his death, Nannie saved nearly fifty letters of condolence coming from all over the country as far north as Bethlehem, Pennsylvania, to as far south as Montgomery, Alabama, personal and business related. He was certainly a respected and loved man.

That love transferred to his children and grandchildren. His correspondence with his children especially his daughter Elizabeth Graham Sanders reflected this. He wrote, "The education of my grandchildren is a subject very near my heart…" and offered Cedar Run as a school location.

Many of these female children's signatures especially "Lizzie," "Friel," and Martha's are found in the mansion today on walls, doors, and windows. Their influence forever written in glass in the windows of the upstairs bedroom is also multiplied by the influence they made in the

world away from Cedar Run. Here are a few examples of the
exceptional Graham women.

An interesting story is Martha "Patsy" Peirce Graham (1875-
1948), the daughter of Nannie Tate and Major David Graham. She is the
subject of a paper by Sarah Fried in 2002 of Vanderbilt University in
Nashville, Tennessee. "Patsy" kept a journal of her life beginning on
June 22, 1896, with an entry that, "All Love is sacred, hopeless love
most sacred of all." She referred to her sister Elizabeth as "Sister Lizzie"
and called the Civil War, which ended a decade before she was born as
the "War of Secession." Fried mentions this entry. "Father (Major David
Graham) is always glad to have me with him when he drives out and I
think Mother and Sister are just as glad to have me at home with them
while Charley, Jim, and Robert make over me in their own ways. David
and Sister Lizzie were just lovely to me the day I spent with them. Friel
and William treat me with cool indifference except when it suits their
convenience to do other wise." Over the next year she made eighty-four
entries in her journal before she married William D. Sanders and had
thirteen children. Ten survived to adulthood.

Another exceptional woman in the Graham family was Agnes
Graham Sanders, who married Dr. Herbert Parkes Riley. Agnes received
a Master's Degree from the University of Chicago and taught at the

University of Kentucky. She met her husband, a Ph.D. in Botany, while they were both at Tulane University (1932-38). She celebrated her 100th birthday in 2002 and her husband retired as an Emeritus Professor after teaching in Lexington from 1942 until 1988. Agnes was the daughter of Elizabeth Graham and Edwin Hanson Sanders. Her brothers Andrew Trigg Sanders and Friel Tate Sanders served in World War II. Andrew was a Captain in an Ordnance Regiment in Italy and North Africa. Friel served in China as part of the 23rd Fighter Control Squadron of the 14th Air Force unit.

Still another woman from the family was Martha Peirce McGavock, the daughter of Emily Graham McGavock. She wrote a paper titled *Three Dreams*, which she wrote of the three accomplishments of humankind being the dream of flight, atomic energy and eternal life. Her writings are part of the Graham papers at the University of Virginia.

Nancy "Nannie" Tate Graham lived in the mansion until her death in 1921. The inventory of her estate gives an insight into the wealth assembled by her family. Seven pages of inventory now at the University of Virginia list her belongings by room. In the Library, Bay Window Room adjoining it, Brown Room and bathroom adjoining it were valued at $212.50 taking inflation into account the value of property in these two rooms to the right as you enter the house today would be worth

$2,700. The total value from inside the house was $915 adjusted for

inflation today would be nearly $12,000. Property at a daughter's home

was valued at $788.50 ($10,000 today). The total home value was

$22,000 in today's dollars.

This gives a room to room idea about what life was like if you

lived in the Graham Mansion. For instance, the Library contained the

following.

Mahogany sofa	$35.00
Secretary and book case	40.00
Books	10.00
Walnut sofa	10.00
Center table	2.50
Small marble top table	2.50
Round top table	1.00
Three rocking chairs	10.00
Walnut arm chair	2.00
Large rug	10.00
Four medium rugs	10.00
Three small rugs	5.00
Five wall pictures	2.50
Plaster bust	0.50
Small vase	0.50
Total	$151.50 (1,992.59 today)

Her land value in 1923 was listed as $37,000 ($486,638.71 in

2011) giving Nannie Tate Graham a total value of $38,703.80

(509,047.77 in 2011). The sale of the Graham Forge property and other

lands added another $25,000 for a total of $63,000 (828,601.05).

Nannie and Major David Graham's seventh child, Wytheville Banker James Montgomery Graham and family were the last of the Grahams to live in the home until the 1930s, when they moved into Wytheville.

As if from a book titled descent from glory, the Grahams ended their time at Cedar Run. The last forge of the Grahams operated until 1916 when a flood destroyed it ending nearly a century of iron production along the Cedar Run by the Graham Family.

The Grahams continued to make their mark on the world away from Cedar Run. William Tate Graham, son of David P. and Nannie M. Graham, became a doctor and co-founded the Crippled Children's Hospital in Richmond. He graduated from Hampden-Sydney and University of Virginia Medical School. He studied orthopedic surgery and became the President of the Virginia State Board of Health.

The Grahams accumulated a massive fortune, but they left a legacy in good works as well. One former employee, John Daniel Kirby, served as foreman at the Cedar Run Farm from the 1920s until 1943. He lived in the large white house near the mansion most of his life. He and his wife, Laeuna, were born and lived most of their lives at Cedar Run Farm. According to his granddaughter, he said, "the Grahams all had a heart for the less fortunate."

Chapter Six
A Family Photo Album

This chapter contains photos of the Graham family and their home before 1943 when it passed from their family. Below, two of Major David Graham's daughters on the front porch.

Mary Bell Graham Matthews, sister of Major David Graham.

Nannie Montgomery Tate Graham, wife of Major David Graham.

Nannie Tate Graham, wife of Major David Graham

Emily Graham McGavock, sister of Major David Graham

Above, Patsy and Friel Graham. Below, left, Marie Matthews and right, Friel Graham.

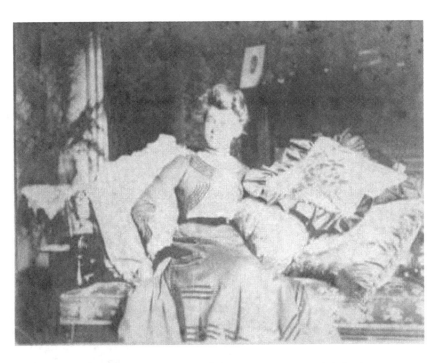

Above, Friel Graham, and below, Patsy and Friel Graham.

Major David Graham on the right with his wife Nannie, center, and daughter, Friel, with two servants.

Above, Robert Graham, Mary Bell Robinson, Ephram McGavock,
Elizabeth Robinson, James Graham and below Patsy and Friel Graham

Lizzie, left, and Friel Graham, right, as babies

Major David Peirce Graham

Friel and Lizzie Graham, above, grandchildren of Nannie and Major
David Graham, below.

John Robinson, husband of Elizabeth Anne Graham.

Mary Bell, sister of Major David Graham.

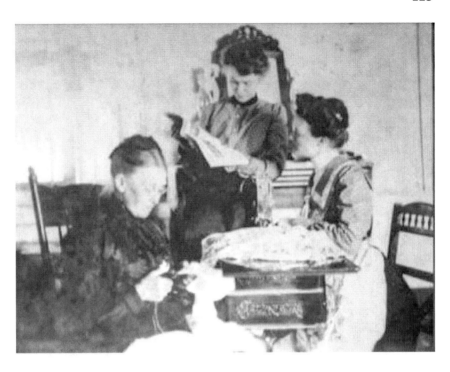

Above, Nannie Tate Graham and two of her daughters. Below,
descendants of Bettie and John Robinson.

Nannie Tate Graham and her grandchildren above and with her children below.

Nannie Tate Graham

The Cedar Run Gun Club

Squire David Graham

Major David Graham

Judge William Fulton, brother-in-law of David Graham at VMI.

Dick Sanders, brother-in-law of Major David Graham.

Major David Graham

William McGavock, brother-in-law of Major David Graham.

Charlie Tate, father-in-law of Major David Graham.

Charles Graham

William H. Tate, brother-in-law of Major David Graham.

Dr. William Tate Graham, son of Major David Graham.

James Tate, brother-in-law of Major David Graham.

Robert Graham, son of Major David Graham.

Jim Graham, son of Major David Graham.

Ed Sanders

Elizabeth "Bettie" Robinson

Mary Bell Graham, Elizabeth Robinson, Julia Graham,
and Jouet McGavock.

The Robinson House, today the W. W. Ranch House.

Reid Stanger Fulton

Chapter Seven
Reid Stanger Fulton

On July 13, 1921, the Des Moines, Iowa, *Evening Tribune* reported that three unmasked bandits and one driver robbed the Drake Park Bank in Des Moines getting away with over $7,000 in cash and Liberty Bonds and escaped in a big powered touring car. The bold daylight raid occurred at 10:10 a.m., but there was one almost hero from the incident. Reid S. Fulton, a professor at nearby Drake University attempted to foil the robbery and for that he received a blow to the back of his head and was "seriously hurt and weakened from loss of blood" and "feared his skull is fractured." Two of the robbers dragged Fulton into a closet in the bank after assaulting him.

After reading this chapter, the reader might wonder if the blow to his skull affected Fulton, but here is report of the robbery written by him while bandaged in the X-Ray room of the hospital. "About 10:15 o'clock I went to the bank where I kept my account. Both the screen and the other doors were closed. I thought it was peculiar for all doors of the bank to be closed in such hot weather. I opened the screen door and then pushed the other door half way open, when someone grabbed me from the inside. He was dressed in Khaki overalls. His face was sunburned and he looked more like a farm hand than a bank robber. He was about 5 feet

6 inches tall and weighed about 160 pounds. I struggled with him. He shouted for me to get into the vault. I fought him off. He pulled a gun from his pocket, but before he could pull the trigger I grabbed the weapon with both hands. Then one of the robbers, this one dressed in a gray suit, came over to my assailant's aid. He hit me over the head with a gun and then both dragged me over to a closet in the bank. I had not been there more than a minute when I head shouts of 'Bank Robbery.' By the time I could manage to stagger from the closet the whole thing was over. The robbers had fled. The whole thing transpired in less than three minutes. The third gun man did not pay any attention to me but continued to work near the vault. I could identify either of my assailants very easily. In fact I am almost positive that I have seen one of the men in the neighborhood before. I had a knife in my pocket and pulled this out to use in case the robbers hit me again but no further attention was paid me after I was dragged through the vault and into the closet."

Founded in 1881 by a "maverick preacher and a swashbuckling Civil War general," Drake University was home to Reid Fulton for three years when the bank robbery occurred. The local newspaper noted his profile rising in the minds of the female population this way. "Prof. R. S. Fulton, dean of the commerce department of Drake University, young, good looking and a bachelor, is even more a target for the admiring view of Drake coeds since his heroic encounter with the bandits. Drake campus fluttered all afternoon with feminine gossip about the professor's handiwork. Fulton himself with a cracked head was unromantically peeved and grumpily uncommital. 'Heroic nothing! I'd liked to have beened a couple of those guys before they got me!' said he. Which is no way for a professor of business English to talk."

Fulton identified "Babe" Emerson in August as one of the robbers. Fulton's actions are explained as Miss Edna Carter, a student, and Mrs. Gladys Stribling and her two children, who were present in the bank. This heroic and eccentric college professor was the first non-Graham owner of the Cedar Run Farm midway through the twentieth century.

Reid Stanger Fulton was born in Grayson County, Virginia, on September 4, 1886, the son of a lawyer turned farmer in Carsonville, just west of Galax along the New River, who served in the Virginia Legislature. Fulton finished his education around 1910. He claimed it started at the Dublin Institute in Pulaski County before matriculating to the University of Virginia where he said he won the "Latin Prize" and was "considered among the most intelligent students ever to attend," but he did not finish at UVA. Instead, he went to Michigan, where he received a BA and then a Master's Degree. Next came a Ph.D. from Columbia University in New York City, which he received while teaching at Drake University. In between his post-graduate degrees, he spent time as a high school principal, taught at Culver Military Institute and the School of Oratory at the University of Michigan.

In 1920, the Trans-Siberian Railroad was just four years old running nearly 6,000 miles from Moscow in Russia to Vladivostok in Siberia. Traveling across the seven different time zones that the train traversed was Reid Stanger Fulton. He claimed he visited six continents including walks across the Alps in Austria and the Pyrenees between France and Spain. He became one of the colorful and in many ways, the saddest owner of the Graham Mansion. Fulton once said he looked like Winston Churchill, but later in life an article described him as a "dark and wizened gnome with a chisel for a nose."

A Drake University publication in 1921 describes Fulton this way. "As director of the School of Commerce, Reid Stanger Fulton needs no introduction to the students of Drake University. He is frequently seen on the campus with his strong, rubbed face set in its stern, purposeful lines, going about his work, giving those of his acquaintance a quick greeting and going quietly past those who are not in his inner circle of friends." He taught salesmanship, statistics and foreign trade at Drake. He lived in a $40 a month flat, discarding furniture on the sidewalks and living with live turkeys before one memorable Thanksgiving. He played handball and had the nickname of "Steamboat." Described as a "man of sartorial elegance," or wearing "flop house clothes," he wore double breasted suits, white shirts, black bow tie, flat brimmed outdated Panama hats, and double heeled shoes to make him taller than his five foot frame.

"While Mr. Fulton admires the man who comports himself with dignity and carries out this idea in himself, he can appreciate a joke and a ludicrous situation as well as the more merrily inclined of his students. The Dean proved his efficiency as a Dean of Commerce last fall when the prices of the books used by the students in his college went almost beyond reach. He bought the books himself and retailed them at cost to his pupils and others in the school, affecting a very material saving in the cost the ultimate consumer of knowledge."

In 1943, Reid Fulton, the eccentric professor from the University of Michigan, Drake University, City College of New York and Columbia University via Independence, Virginia, who had a PhD in Economics, purchased the twenty-five room Graham Mansion and the surrounding 735 acres for $70,000. His original purpose was to buy the timber, but he sold the trees for $100,000, kept the property, and began to spend his summers at the home. In 1957 or 1959 depending on the source, he retired from teaching at City College of New York and came home to the Graham Mansion in Wythe County and an expanded 1,300 acres.

Before retiring, he came to Wythe County on the train from New York City to Pulaski, Virginia during the summers and long breaks from teaching. He then caught a ride on the Star Route Mail Truck on the U. S. Post Office for eighteen miles to Max Meadows with "sandwiches and two satchels of books." He paid 50 to 75 cents for the ride until it went up to a dollar. After that he walked carrying his satchels one at a time for a few hundred yards and then go back and get the other, which one writer estimated took him over twenty-four hours to get from Pulaski to his home.

He sold timber off the land to have money and refused to pay wages. Doing "everything with a two bit axe" and describing himself as a "unreconstructed mercantilist," Fulton lived with no running water and without electricity until the 1970s. Fulton said that "by abandoning the superfluous survival values" such as running water, he eliminated the "bugaboos of daily living' and became very rich.

Reid Fulton lived alone and miserly saving his money so he could collect books, lots of books. His hoarding of books took on obsessive behavior. He reportedly once canceled a ship passage from England to the United States just to buy a basement full of books. He culled the valuable volumes and sold the rest as scrap. Fulton became known for his massive, 70,000-volume antique book collection, which filled the mansion from floor to ceiling. Visitors reported walking through narrow paths lit by four "sooty" hurricane lamps surrounded by "books, tools, rags, bottles, boxes, tires, lumber, and cans of motor oil." It is a miracle that one spark did not cause a hurricane of fire ending the existence of the hermit and the house he lived. Apparently, some thought less of some books as they had bullet holes in them.

Paraphrasing from a Fulton interview where he mentioned it, being a millionaire has its advantages. You can marry the boss's charming daughter, not greasy cook, live in a big house, and never work while riding in a big car. According to Katherine Kirby Akers of Ft. Chiswell, Katherine's older sister Roberta Kirby was born in the nearby split-level log house (now the Chimney House Stage foundation at the Graham Mansion) in 1921. According to Mrs. Akers, Reid Fulton and her aunt Roberta shared "a strong romantic interest," but "they did not marry out of faith."

Fulton's eccentric or just plain weird behavior became the thing of legend locally with various sources reporting that Fulton lived at the mansion without electricity, telephone, running water or central heat. It is said, "He ate buzzard eggs and bathed in Cedar Run." His diet apparently included "discontinued" canned food or boiling a dead, fully intact possum for dinner guests. He ate nothing frozen and only fresh meat. Fulton believed that "meat eaters build empires" while "vegetarians never conqueror" anything. He did not bathe at the mansion, as there was no running water, but traveled to his sister's home for baths. He cooked over an open fire with a long handled skillet. He drank water in plastic jugs from his nephew's well in Grayson County. He said the limestone water at the mansion hurt his kidneys. He greeted visitors at the front door with his shotgun. Supposedly, he roamed the mansion "buck naked or clothed in nothing but an old raincoat and boots." He charged children ten cents a gallon to pick berries. Hunters gave half their kills to the owner of the property for the privilege of hunting the property. He got so much venison that he rented freezers in Wytheville to store it.

He drove an old two-ton International Harvester 1600 Loadstar truck without the truck bed that cost fifty cents a mile to drive. He welded an I-beam to the front. Fulton thought it was the closest thing he could find to a tank as he was afraid of death on the highway. He owned four trucks and three tractors that he drove until 1977. He disliked driving and once turned down a new Cadillac for his books because the "depreciation would bring a loss."

One source tells this story. "Emily Swanger visited the mansion as a young girl. Swanger is granddaughter of Samuel Frye, previous vice-mayor of Pulaski and nephew of Reid Fulton. Frye was also the executor of Fulton's estate. When visiting the mansion, Swanger's grandmother made her wear white gloves and she was forbidden to touch anything or sit on the furniture. She confirms what has long-been rumored, stating, 'everything you have heard about Reid Fulton is true!"

She adds that Fulton, who never married, bought the mansion because "he wanted to have a house that was bigger than his brother's!' " His brother Paul inherited the family home place, "much to Reid's dislike. When Paul died, Reid bought a larger headstone for his own grave just to have a bigger headstone and a bigger house.

He spent his time reading and sleeping at the mansion and another home in Grayson County. He spoke of his life. "The silence can be music and a beautiful lesson. I awake long before daylight and can determine its approach by the motor vehicles outside. Keeping time confuses me I can't remember the days." He often walked to a nearby bank before it opened dressed in a worn overcoat and a white shirt with "two exquisite pistols for protection." No doubt, this came from his experience trying to stop a bank robbery in 1921.

He spoke of "Silent Influences" keeping a composition book with the great men who have departed for "The Land of Memory." He said, "When we remember that these renowned characters, made so by the brilliancy of achievements, slumber in eternity, the soul trembles with a touch of melancholy as a harp whose saddening notes die in plaintive echoes when swept by the wander breeze."

His existence was lonely and sad. One writer reported finding him sitting quietly alone by a coal stove one bitter cold night reading Plato beneath an oil lamp with a head of cabbage boiling beside him. He often bought food in bulk that spoiled before he ate it. He canned peaches and beans and let his house go from being a "regional showplace" to looking like a set from Erskine Caldwell's *Tobacco Road*. There was no telephone and he never used the furnace. He did his own labor stating, "Men let themselves grow soft. We have produced a nation of weaklings. Omit the exercising and poisons penetrate the tissues, opening the way for invasions of diseases."

He bound books or maybe rebound books or built bookshelves from the lumber on the property. Many book collectors came to visit learning via "word of mouth" about Fulton. His collection contained "No Fiction" and few novels except Thackeray were "worth having." He said it was an economic and not a literary assessment. His collection had no catalog and dated from before 1500. He spent hundreds of dollars or as little as $2.50 for a book. He said he would destroy his library rather than let it fall into hands of the communists. He bought books from auctions, estate sales, shops, attics, courthouses, and other collectors. Books were stored in the barn, washhouse, springhouse, boiler room and even a warehouse in New York City before he retired. "I collected books with care, for sheer pleasure and possible edification." He reported selling his collection on transportation to the Henry Ford Library for $25,000 and claimed that Emory and Henry College bought 1,500 volumes on Americana.

Reid S. Fulton's grandfather, Creed Fulton, was a founder of Emory and Henry College. A 1914 observatory on campus bears his name. The Fulton ties to southwest Virginia and education were strong, but not everyone had a high opinion of Fulton and his care of his book collection. J. Allen Neal of Emory and Henry College reported one story of Fulton arriving at the small Methodist College asking to see the President of the college to sell a book. It was a two volume history published in Mexico from 1515. Emory and Henry College purchased many volumes, but reported that Fulton had "no real love of what he had collected. It seemed to be only for the money." Neal reported that during a visit to the mansion that Fulton "paused and picked up a book that was nearly priceless. He was holding it by the cover and it ripped in half. He just tossed it down on the floor and went on." Duke University described his library as "overpriced vanilla." Another said Fulton would "toss a $200 book on the floor and use it as a step stool to reach some other book. Rain and snow are ruining valuable books out in the barn, but Fulton doesn't seem to care."

It seems whenever a regional newspaper needed a story they came to see Reid S. Fulton. These stories recount some of his philosophy on life and his theories on the world and famous people who interested him. When he was 91 a story titled "Eccentric Book Hoarder Living Last Days in Filth" by Bill McKelway described Fulton as living a "final act of eccentric detachment." Fulton told McKelway of his book collection, "My young man you see before you the largest collection of literature ever assembled by a single member of humankind. What do you desire to purchase?"

Newsweek described him as preaching "McKinley era economics" and "If he excelled at anything academic, it was in taking attendance." The same article described Fulton as nailing a second heel on a shoe to save wear and tear on the sole with the ominous warning that when "a man starts something like that and it gets to be a habit."

For instance, Fulton said that Napoleon Bonaparte's Marshal Ney escaped after Waterloo and came to North Carolina and taught school in Salisbury. Plato, Karl Marx, and the French Statesman Turgot were the only real philosophers the world produced worth considering. Only two "runts" made it big in history and they were Napoleon and King David. Flavius Josephus was the world's greatest historian. He made himself and the Roman Empire famous and never once mentioned Jesus Christ, which Fulton felt proved Jesus never existed. Of course, even a visit to Wikipedia will tell the reader that Josephus did mention Jesus. "Now there was about this time Jesus, a wise man, if it be lawful to call him a man; for he was a doer of wonderful works, a teacher of such men as receive the truth with pleasure. He drew over to him both many of the Jews and many of the Gentiles. He was [the] Christ." Fulton thought that life after death was a "pipedream."

Economics was a favorite subject. He lectured his farmer neighbors about their faulty economics discussing implicit and explicit rent. He told one neighbor while "smiling wickedly," "I'll tell you why you can't make any money on those cattle you bought, but you might want to go out and commit suicide after I do." He did not like the economic policies of Franklin D. Roosevelt, which would lead to the "total destruction of the nation." He felt the nation was on the brink of total communism, which he thought was bad as it "could have been invented by anyone with the mind of a twelve year old."

He thought the Lincoln Assassination was a "Catholic Conspiracy" and that Booth was innocent and escaped to Grayson County. Custer disobeyed orders at the Little Big Horn and it cost him his life and the future Presidency of the United States. Fulton said, "all mistakes in English can be divided into three categories: barbarism, socialism and impropriety."

Reid Fulton's ownership of the mansion and grounds continued until the late 1970s. He spent most of his time in the kitchen area near the wood stove. One interview described him wearing a suit coat, pair of shoes and like almost everything in the house covered by a layer of coal dust. While buzzards circled over the "ornate wrought iron railings atop the angular gables" of the house right out of a Hitchcock movie or an episode from Scooby Doo, Fulton lived on in the Graham Mansion. His

books gathered cobwebs and the already mentioned coal dust while rats

"scurry boldly over furniture in quest of decaying morsels of food."

Fulton had a bed, stuffed chair, and stepladder to keep him company.

COUNTY AND STATE POLICE OFFICERS were out in full force late yesterday afternoon, following the theft of books from the home of Reid Fulton at Graham's Forge. The TOP photo shows the police officers in the lane that leads to the Fulton house. In foreground, the first of the accused thieves arrested, George Nelson Reynolds, is in the Sheriff's car, while Deputy Billy May and Trooper Brooks secure information, age, etc. from Reynolds. The 22-year-old Blacksburg area youth was arrested in the barn in foreground. The other three alleged accomplices were arrested later last night.

Fulton's life as a crime fighter continued in later years. Not

everyone was willing to let Fulton and his collection live in peace. He

once surprised two thieves and delivered them himself to the Sheriff at

gunpoint. Fulton got another chance to be a crime fighter fifty-seven

years after trying to foil a bank robbery in Iowa. In March 1978, after apparently learning of Fulton's collection of a "million books" in the

Roanoke newspaper, four young people with last names of Reynolds,

Long, Price, and even Graham all aged 23 years tried to steal books from

the collection in multiple break ins. Deputies observed one of the culprits

carrying books down a nearby road to a parked car. When approached,

he ran into the carriage house and was "flushed" from his hiding place.

Law enforcement tracked the other "trio" into a nearby barn, but did not

use tear gas, as the structure was empty. The books valued at $20,000

were recovered.

Fulton claimed he sold the property for half a million dollars to Dr. James L. Chitwood of Pulaski in 1974 (Another report was $400,000), but retained lifetime rights to live in the house. He bought a home in Wytheville for $35,000 in 1976. Reid Stanger Fulton said he would live to 100, but he died on September 21, 1979, and is buried in the Reid Fulton Cemetery near Fallville in his native Grayson County.

In 1984, Dr. Chitwood worked to have the home and twenty-one acres of the 1,300 acres he owned placed on the Virginia Landmarks Register and the National Register of Historic Places. Chitwood purchased part of Fulton's library for $30,000. It contained 1,500 crates with 60,000 volumes and 10,000 pamphlets that took eighteen months of cataloging after Chitwood sold it to Virginia Tech.

Reid Fulton and Dr. James Chitwood in the Graham Mansion.

Dr. James Chitwood, above in the Graham Mansion and below, at one of the surviving furnaces.

Josiah Cephas Weaver

Chapter Eight
Josiah Cephas Weaver

On November 14, 2010, this author, J. W. Smith, and Josiah C. Weaver found ourselves listening to AM 1280 out of Wytheville, Virginia, to the morning gospel show hosted by the electrician, Jerry Stone, who worked for Weaver at the Graham Mansion. We came together that day for an event at the site involving Civil War reenactors and tours of the house. Spending any time with Josiah C. Weaver is to encounter a force of nature. Described as a man who "speaks his mind, and holds tight to his beliefs with a huge heart. If you can keep up with him." He is a man full of life who often says, "To me life is beautiful and I am thankful for every day on God's Earth." That morning we listened to different artists singing I Saw The Light, Will The Circle Be Unbroken and some of Josiah's own songs. During the conversation, talk turned to Weaver's home along Yellow Mountain Road in southern Roanoke County.

Two months before the Japanese bombed Pearl Harbor, Hawaii, sending the United States into World War II, Josiah Cephas Weaver saw the light, the first light of life on October 9, 1941. Born to Geneva and Elmer Weaver, Josiah remembers at the age of five sweeping at his father's sawmill and passing out water to the workers. At age eight, he was driving the Ford log truck "turning logs." By age twelve, he was driving with his father in 1953 Oldsmobile to Florida to bird hunt and camp out.

Life for Weaver involved hard work. He did play football, but his father disapproved, so he worked instead of having fun. He cut wood all day at neighbors. Being one of nine children, he learned self-reliance. Weaver became a "quick study" observing human nature that has paid off with dividends throughout his life. Weaver's relative "Price Bandy" was developmentally disabled. He looked normal, but could not read. Weaver said Bandy was the "smartest man I ever knew." Today, Weaver raises money for the Clearwater UPARC in Bandy's honor. Weaver said that Bandy could track honeybees through the woods, smoke them out, and never get stung. He grew vegetables and sold them at the Roanoke market square. Josiah's father treated him differently than his other children. Seeing something in the young man, he pushed his son. His father passed in 1964 of stomach cancer. Josiah believed it was due to the DDT and chemicals used on the farm. Growing up just south of Roanoke in Virginia, Weaver picked Granny Smith apples for his mother's cobblers, gardened, sold tomatoes on the Roanoke Market Square, and kept the fire in her wood stove going when not milking the cows. He walked barefoot to Garden City Elementary

Josiah Cephas Weaver

School, and skinny-dipped with his brother, Maynard, in the cool waters of Back Creek. Weaver says that family, church, school, and work were the "rocks" of his young life, but music was his life's water.

The music washed away the dirt of life, immersed him in the language of the hills, and fed his childhood dreams and dream he did indeed. From his earliest memories, Josiah sang songs. For almost sixty years, Josiah created songs to entertain just about anyone who would listen. Josiah sang songs to tell stories about life and somewhere along the line taught himself to play the guitar and piano. To this day, he cannot read or write music, but never really had a need to learn! On Sunday afternoons, his Uncle Brandon Hartman came over with his "ole GEEtar" and fiddle, sat out on the back porch swing, ate fried chicken legs "like they was nothing" and the music flowed like the quick current of the nearby Roanoke River.

After putting in a long summer day at the sawmill, Josiah and his cousin Price Bandy drank Orange Crush outside the Hidey Ho Country Store and sang along with Hank Williams on the radio. On a Saturday night you might find Josiah and Bobby Hylton headed up to the Starkey Speedway, cruising in a '37 "Flying 8" Ford coupe. Although the Weaver family home did not have electricity or indoor plumbing during those early years, Josiah felt his harsh childhood provided a solid foundation that fed his flow of music for "'bout near" 6 decades.

Josiah's childhood ended quickly when at the age 15 when he left home alone. After an accident with his father's logging truck, Josiah left his home at the foot of the Blue Ridge Mountains and headed south. He saved his hard-earned money and took a Greyhound bus to Tampa, Florida. When he arrived with only a few quarters left in the pockets of his Wrangler jeans, he walked 20 miles to Clearwater. That first night he slept in a phone booth. "I didn't know mosquitoes come as big as I saw that night."

He did not look back. He left home daily at 4 a.m. and returned by midnight. He found work as a tile-setter apprentice and by the age of 19 started Weaver Tile Company. For the next 20 years, Weaver Tile flourished in central Florida and by the mid-1970s, Josiah was building warehouses and offices for lease in Clearwater, where he had visited as a youth with his father on their hunting trips. By 1978, he closed his tile business and set his sights on the development of Weaver Enterprises including Weaver Park, which today includes approximately 400,000 square feet of leased office and warehouse space in Clearwater. "I just went down to Florida and built a shopping center."

His secretary/bookkeeper from 1969 until 2001, Marilyn Cantrell from Guilford County, North Carolina, has a different view of her former boss. She describes him as a multiprocessor working with the tile company, and industrial park while writing songs in his head. Weaver is the quintessential "self-made man" living the "American Dream." He "expected the best" and was very hands on and very willing to do the "heavy lifting."

This man taught himself to fly planes and helicopters without reading instructions and worked with heavy earth moving equipment to move earth. Weaver does not need much sleep working thirty-six hours with six hours of sleep he is back at it for another thirty-six. He cultivated the company of older men such as Jack Eckert, who started Eckert Drug Stores, John Jenkins, who started Publix with his brother George, or Bud Paxton and Roy Spears who started in a studio at Weaver Park what became the Home Shopping Network, now QVC.

Many grand gentlemen owned the Graham Mansion over the years including Reid S. Fulton, who sold the Graham Mansion to Dr. James Chitwood, who made much-needed repairs such as shoring up the original frame section. A corporation from West Virginia owned the property briefly before the gentleman from Franklin County via Florida Josiah Cephus Weaver purchased the property in 1989. The Graham

Land adjoined his W.W. Ranch, which was once part belonged to the Grahams. He created a 4000-acre tract sandwiched between Interstates 77 and 81. Weaver maintained the mansion and surrounding buildings including a house where various supervisors over the years lived to protect the mansion from disrepair and vandalism. The W. W. Ranch raises Angus and Hereford beef cattle.

In 2006, Weaver cleared the collapsed Carriage House debris to reveal a beautiful limestone foundation. Josiah then leveled up the ancient foundation and resurrected it to become a stage for events at the mansion. As Josiah Weaver continued to make visible repairs, carloads of interested people stopped to visit the mansion and ask about the history. It was then, during that hot summer of 2006, Josiah decided to host a yearly music festival there, thus opening the mansion to the public for the very first time.

Today when he is not overseeing Weaver Enterprises, Josiah can often be found at his beloved W.W. Ranch near Wytheville, Virginia that includes the Graham Mansion. On any given day he may be checking his Hereford and Angus herds, hunting wild turkey or deer, clearing land with his Cat 955 "dozer," making up songs as Stevie Barr picks his banjo on the side porch, or telling jokes with his ranch foreman, J.W. Smith, and his nephew and ranch assistant, Rayven "Razor" Weaver.

Every year you can find Josiah C. Weaver at GrahamFest doing what he loves, doing what flows naturally, singing, and entertaining the people who mean the most to him in the hills of his Virginia home. In July 2006, J. C. Weaver hosted his first annual July 4th party at the newly rebuilt Carriage House Foundation Stage. Weaver rebuilt the Mansion front porch and preserved the original cast iron columns. This begins his dream of hosting a music festival at the historic property.

The following year during Labor Day Weekend on September 3, 2007, Weaver hosted his first GrahamFest Music Festival with over 3000 in attendance. The following month the Virginia Paranormal Society began to investigate local reports of paranormal activity at the Major Graham's Mansion. The group confirmed what many locals believed that the Mansion is haunted.

On August 31 and September 1, 2008, Weaver hosted his GrahamFest Music Festival and again the following year. Beginning in 2010, GrahamFest "moved back" to July 4.

Weaver's performing music life goes back over six decades. Josiah formed his first band, The Neptunes in the mid-50s. His first songs were released on 45 records. On several occasions The Neptunes were the opening act for touring shows including Florida performances by Johnny Cash and Conway Twitty. In the 1960s, Weaver formed Wild

Turkey Music, Inc. to record and produce his own songs.

In the 1980s, he had twelve songs in the top 100 on Cash Box

Magazine's country charts, many of them written and recorded in his

"little white rock house recording studio" previously located on what is

now Josiah Cephas Weaver Park in Dunedin, Florida. In 1980, Josiah

and the Florida Symphony Orchestra performed one of his "rock house

songs," "America, God's People Love You" in St. Petersburg for then

presidential candidate Ronald Reagan. In 1986, Josiah penned another

"rock house song" in memory of an 18 year old Dunedin friend and

soldier, who died in Vietnam. That song, "Salute the Boys of Vietnam,"

was recognized in the Congressional Record on October 16th of that same

year by Senator Sasser from Tennessee. In 1991, Cash Box Magazine

selected Josiah as the Top Male Country Vocalist in the Independent

Artist category. His song, "Girls That Look a Little Like You" remained

number one on the charts for two consecutive weeks.

Mountain Rock Music is Josiah's first passion, but NASCAR

runs a very close second. In 1988, Josiah was the proud owner of the

Ford Thunderbird called the "Music Machine," which ran in three

NASCAR Cup races. His racing theme song, "Feeling Good," was

ranked #83 on the Cash Box charts as his car was being clocked for the

Daytona 500. As owner and sponsor of the NASCAR Nextel #58 Monte Carlo in 2007, Josiah sponsored childhood friend 72-year-old James Hylton at Daytona 500.

Weaver bought this two-year-old car, leased an engine from Richard Childress Racing Inc., and went to work. He started slow, but improved. Weaver coached the driver saying "pretend you are running in the hills of Yellow Mountain Road along Back Creek in Roanoke County, Virginia," where they both grew up.

Over the years, Josiah Weaver wrote thousands of songs and produced them on 45 records, albums, cassette tapes, and compact discs. Josiah released five original CDs after 1994. They are "Country Rock 'N Roll" (1995), "Crossing Over" (1998), "Winning Colors" (2005), and "Comin' Home" (2009). These songs are available on CDs or as single song download at www.cdbaby.com/jcweaver.

Whether Josiah is performing with Charlie Daniels and friends at his annual Charliepalooza event at the Tampa Hard Rock Casino (2006), in front of 25,000 screaming Market America supporters at the Greensboro Coliseum (2009), or just making up a song for an old friend who is sick, he is ever mindful of what is important and dear in life. (See www.YouTube.com/JCWeaver)

In 2008 Josiah, the Florida Land Trust, Florida Forever, Pinellas County, and the city of Dunedin finalized the transfer of his waterfront home and 14 acres of inland and submerged land, to the opened in 2011 Josiah Cephas Weaver Park. Josiah continues to manage the Clearwater property he designed and built over the past 30 years, Weaver Industrial Park.

From his youth to his earliest days in Florida to the present, Josiah Weaver's river of music flowed. In fact, when life was the toughest, when he worked for 36 straight hours laying tile and supervising over 100 employees, when his much loved wife passed away from cancer in 1980, when the future was hard to see, it was his steady core faith in God, and his mountain music that carried his soul to the next day, to the next level, and carry him it did to the Graham Mansion and the pages of this book.

"I've always had this dream in my head. The dream kept telling me to preserve the history and the beauty of this land. The dream keeps telling me to share the music. My dream is now GrahamFest."

Josiah C. Weaver might sum his philosophy on life this way. "Good times, hard work, living good, staying in the straight course and let's enjoy life...I ain't had no hang ups and no holdbacks. Let's Roll!"

"My dream always brings me back home. Back home to my Virginia roots. Back to my ranch and this old mansion in Southwest Virginia. Back to taking care of the past and building for tomorrow." Thanks to Josiah for living his dream and preserving this little place of history in Wythe County, Virginia. One of the pleasures of writing this book is getting to know this self made man and Mary Lin Brewer, for whom this book is dedicated as she is now the lady of the house at the Graham Mansion.

Afterword
A House On A Hill

Today many members of the Graham Family rest today in a
family cemetery on a high hill across Virginia Route 626 from the
mansion they once called home. Still owned by the Graham Family, this
is the last resting place of the family that built the large house on the
opposite hill and left their mark on the history of Wythe County and this
nation.

Those who followed have left a colorful and interesting story as
well. This house sits within sight of Interstate Highway I-77 running
north and south from Ohio to South Carolina at mile marker 29 from the
Virginia/North Carolina boundary line near a red roofed barn that seems
to be asking someone to paint "See Rock City" on it. If you did not
notice the red barn, you might not even look to the east and see in the
distance the enormous house this book speaks of, but if you did the size
of the house would astound you.

The first time I, like many people, saw it was from gravel road
Virginia Route 619 traveling on Major Graham's Road from Highway 52
just north of the New River and Jackson's Ferry, it took my breath away.
I came searching for the Graham Mansion while trying to follow in the
footsteps of J. E. B. Stuart for another project. I came around the curve
and saw the massive structure high up on a hill above Cedar Run
looming as an enormous shadow on the country side as its history casts a
similar shadow on the history of the region and the nation.

PART TWO
A GUIDE

This section is a guide to the Graham Mansion pointing out the architectural significance of the house and outbuildings that make it a special place. The mansion has twenty-five rooms and 11,000 square feet. The original, rear frame section of the Mansion was built in the 1830s and the huge, formal brick section was added in the 1850s. Later, Major David Graham added another addition to the structure completing the mansion as seen today.

As one neighbor once said, "that old place has been haunted ever since I can remember. We been-a seein' lights, faces in the winders, hearin' strange noises, and I even hear tell-a folks finding see through circles on theys pictures. My granddaddy showed me that hickory tree up on that hill yonder where them slaves were hanged for killin' theys master long time ago."

The Graham Mansion is haunted or so says many local paranormal societies. The guide will incorporate some of the stories in the following pages.

Phase One circa 1830

These two views of the original section of the mansion built by Squire David Graham. Tradition states this part of the house contains the log structure of the Bakers.

The Georgian Side Porch facing Cedar Run is the original entrance. This pillared portico reflects a definite Charleston influence. Notice the intricate woodwork and rope trim around the door.

The original dumb waiter in the adjacent windowed workroom going up to the Hearth Room. This is located in the 1830s Graham house, so that food brought from the nearby by kitchen could be raised to the Hearth Room for preparation before serving during the summer. A winter kitchen is located on the ground level through the window shown here.

The room used today as the kitchen was originally the "hearth room," a combination living room and dining room. The hearth room is anchored by a huge fireplace, which is framed by an ornate mahogany fireplace mantle and the functional nearby warming oven located in the radiators shown on the next page. It is one of twelve fireplaces in the house.

Since the frame and brick sections were built separately and at different time periods, the basements are not connected and there are two staircases. Here are photos of the staircase from the oldest part of the house. The rear stairway woodwork is original. A glance upward reveals a beautiful view of the decorative scrollwork.

The rear second floor bedroom is the site of Bettie Graham's Civil War era schoolroom. This is also the room that a "clairvoyant" encountered "Clara," an orphan from the time of the Civil War, who Emily and Bettie Graham kept and tutored her with the other children. When Squire David Graham discovered the presence of "Clara" he strongly disapproved, but the girl died of tuberculosis or pneumonia.

      The third floor "Secret Confederate Meeting Room" was most likely used as a child's bedroom. Local legend has it that Confederate officers met secretly in this very room and wounded soldiers were tended to in the adjacent attic.

Here are two gothic like images of the Graham Mansion from the twentieth century.

Phase Two 1850s

The second phase of the Graham Mansion began under the management of Squire David Graham starting in the early 1850s and completed in 1855-56. When you enter the house there are two large rooms on either side of the entrance hall and staircase with four large fireplaces. Two large rooms to the right, the parlor and dining room are separated by massive double doors. To the left are the library and family room. The second floor contains four bedrooms, which one was later enclosed to create a small fifth bedroom.

To the left as you enter the Graham Mansion is the library. The downstairs parlor and study feature arched, highly ornate mahogany doorways leading to the side Victorian sun porches, which were part of the third and fourth phases completed by Major David Graham in the 1870s and 1890s.

Over the years, much of the original glass, doors, decorative tile, light fixtures, and woodwork have been vandalized. It is Josiah Weaver's hope that opening the Mansion to the public during events will eliminate these unfortunate events.

Major David Graham completed Phase Three and Four of the Graham Mansion adding dormers, a slate roof, bow windows before 1898. The decorative grillwork is actually wood, but looks like iron. The last section contains rose-colored brick. The four pillars on a small front porch were cast iron made on the property and painted white to resemble wood.

The Victorian porches contain some rather unique windows and no doors! These elongated windows have three stacked panes, which open to create a doorway for porch access. In the 19th century, some southern homes were taxed based on the number of exterior doors, thus the creation of the "window door"!

As visitors walk across the deep door thresholds between the original frame house and formal brick "addition," a contrast in building style, workmanship, and scale is apparent. The brick mansion addition boasts massive rooms, plain wood trim details, and elaborate exterior workmanship.

Known as the Parlor, today this room displays the musical career of Josiah C. Weaver.

The Entrance Hall looks towards the front door. Notice the door to the basement to the right and the ever present deer. Below, looking from the front door.

The Living Room and Dining Rooms span the length of the brick addition. These rooms are separated by massive floor-to-ceiling oak doors!

Second Floor

As visitors continue up the massive, elegant mahogany staircase and across the foyer's heart of pine floors, it is difficult to imagine the daily maintenance of this home over 150 years ago! When you reach the top of the stairs turn to the right for the Christmas Room.

The Christmas Room traditionally was the place the women and children celebrated the holiday and Easter without the men present. The ghost hunters claim this is "the happiest room" in the house as shown below by this author's friend Denise Coalson. Denise and her sister Deb Coalson Bisel, like this author, visited this house on their own many years ago.

Bride's Room

The ghost hunters say that many people have seen a woman in white standing by the window next to the fireplace in this room. Perhaps she is waiting for her husband to return from the Civil War or so the story goes.

Out the window of this room you can see the white house used by caretakers after the Graham's left the mansion. This house, too, is haunted. A recent male resident of the house claimed to see a "lady in a veil," who appeared to him at the bottom of the staircase almost every morning. The lady of the house saw her upstairs, in the front bedroom and once claimed to snap a photo of the veiled lady.

Next door between the Bride's Room and Martha's Room is the Pink Room, which was once part of the landing for the staircase, but was closed off to create another bedroom. It might have been a nursery or a sitting room for Martha Peirce Graham. Sound in this room are amplified possibly due to the cast iron pillars from the front porch outside the window of this small room.

Martha's Room

Do not miss the "Secret Window Bedroom" as it contains a unique windowpane etching. Legend has it that the etching was made by a bride's diamond ring on her wedding night! The lovely cursive letters give us only a few clues….the date, February 24, 1864, 4 sets of initials, and the signature of one of the Graham family members.

This is Martha's Room named for the wife of Squire David Graham. Several people believe due to her mental illness she was locked away when visitors came and scratched her name in the window. This is a good story, but this author believes these etchings are simply the tradition of young girls checking out the caliber of the diamond engagement rings presented by their beaus. M. Bell Peirce is Mary Bell

Peirce, the daughter of James and Nancy Anne Dabney Stuart Peirce. This young lady was the niece of Confederate Major General J. E. B. Stuart and not Martha Peirce Graham.

The ghost hunters say Martha still resides here and is a "restless spirit" and a "prankster," who enjoys making the paranormal investigators "squirm."

The Grahams were clearly ahead of their times! They also used carbide lights and steam heat long before most of their southern (and northern) neighbors!

Fulton Room

Next door to Martha's room is another bedroom used today to denote the time Reid Fulton owned the Graham Mansion. Almost as eccentric as the former owner, Reid Fulton, Josiah Weaver and Mary Lin Brewer have a little fun with the deer collection.

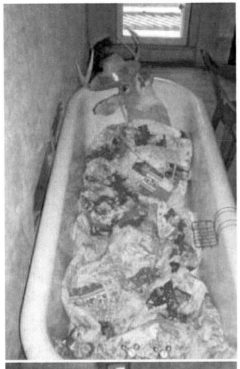

Phase Three and Four

Major David Graham supervised the massive hip-on-hip
replacement slate roof and its ornate tower and dormers in the 1870s as
well as the intricate Victorian porch additions in the late 1800s. An
upward glance reveals a massive slate roof complete with dormers, a
tower, ornate lightning rods, and exquisite Celtic crosses. On the
northernmost side dormer, guests can read the original signature of the
home's Max Meadows builder. The southern exposure yields a
magnificent view of the ante-bellum Victorian porches and woodwork.
The front porch entrance to the Mansion grandly displays its signature,
one-of-a-kind, cast iron columns made at the Cedar Run furnace.
Directly in front of the porch visitors can just imagine ladies in
hoopskirts dismounting their horses by using the huge stepping stone,
placed there for just that purpose.

Outbuildings

A large operation like the Cedar Run Farm required the Grahams to building several supporting buildings. Many of these structures survive until this day.

Wash House

The outbuilding to the left of the porch is the washhouse, which houses the original fire pit, chimney, boiling cauldron, drain, and rinse basin.

You can also view the old ringer washer inside the Wash House.

The Office and Slave Quarters

    The 5-room/3 story outbuilding directly behind the kitchen is the summer kitchen and servants' quarters. The winter kitchen is located in the basement directly beneath the updated first floor indoor kitchen of the mansion. The opposite rear enclosed side porch and storage room date this frame structure as "pre-1850" by virtue of the type of ceiling plaster and lathe work according to local historians. Mansion visitors will notice that this plaster is made from mud and horsehair applied to wooden lathes.

The Spring House

The Spring House to the left with the Chimney House stage to the right in the distance is Interstate 77. GrahamFest uses multiple stages including the Chimney House, Carriage House and the Major Graham stage. The music festival spans genres including country, blue-grass, oldies, rock and roll and is closed each year by Josiah Weaver's Mountain Rock Music Show.

Above, original structures including the barn to the left in the distance is used for food and drink vendors. To the right in the foreground is a barn used during GrahamFest and other events on the grounds of the Graham Mansion as the General Store and as the "Blood Barn" during SpookyWorld. The Carriage House below collapsed in the 1990s and its foundation is now a stage.

Near the house you will find the fish "holding pond" where the Grahams kept freshly caught fish. The Chimney House Stage, located behind the Mansion, is built on the actual foundation of a circa 1800s split level log cabin. In the distance is Interstate 77. Guests are invited to walk the immediate grounds around the Mansion. Please notice the Carriage House Stage, built by Josiah Weaver in the summer of 2006 on its original building foundation.

Graham Family Cemetery

    The Graham Family Cemetery sits across Virginia Route 626 from the Graham Mansion, is private property still owned by the family, and is not part of the W. W. Ranch.

Graves of Squire David and Martha Peirce Graham.

Graham Mansion Chronology

1775: Graham family founder, Robert Graham, immigrates to Wythe County area in 1775 and serves one year in Revolutionary War.

1800: Squire David Graham born.

1835: Squire David Graham marries Martha Bell Peirce; Squire David operates 12 furnaces, a forge, and a grain mill, is part owner of nearby Lead Mines, owns 6,000-8,000 acres in the Grahams Forge community, and is known as the "first ironsmith of southwest Virginia". He begins to build the original rear frame section of the Mansion in the 1830s.

1838: Major David Peirce Graham born at "Cedar Run."

1848: Bricks were made locally for the massive Mansion "addition."

1855: Mansion "addition" completed

1861: Major Graham joins Confederate Army; later discharged due to illness and continues to develop father's iron business and supply pig iron to the war effort.

1868: Major Graham marries Nancy Montgomery Tate.

1870: Mansion 2-story slate roof, towers, and dormers added

1890: Victorian porches and sunrooms added

1930s: Jim Graham, a Wytheville banker and resident of "Cedar Run", moves his family from the Mansion "to town" and uses the property intermittently for holiday and picnic outings.

1943: Home and approximately 1200 acres purchased by law professor Reid Fulton.

1974: Fulton sold the property to Dr. James Chitwood of Pulaski

1984: Dr. Chitwood listed the mansion property on the National Historic Register.

1990: a corporation from West Virginia owned the property briefly before J.C. (Josiah Cephus) Weaver purchased the property in early 1990 and incorporated it into his current 4000 acre W.W. Ranch where he raises Angus and Hereford beef cattle.

July 2006: J.C. "Josiah" Weaver hosts his annual July 4th party at the newly rebuilt Carriage House foundation stage. J.C. also rebuilds the Mansion front porch and preserves its original cast iron columns.

September 3, 2007: Josiah hosts his first GrahamFest Music Festival with over 3000 in attendance.

October 2007: Paranormal investigations begin and later confirm local reports of paranormal activity at the Graham Mansion.

2008: August 31 – September 1, Josiah's inaugural GrahamFest Music Festival.

2009: October, first Graham Mansion Halloween event.

2012: GrahamFest returns on July 4th weekend to raise money for the St. Jude's Children's Hospital.

Web Links

Major Graham's Mansion http://majorgrahammansion.com/

SpookyWorldUSA http://spookyworldusa.com

Weaver's Outdoor World www.VirginiaGuidedHunting.com

Laurel Hill Publishing www.freestateofpatrick.com

Visit Wytheville http://www.visitwytheville.com

Wythe Chamber of Commerce http://www.wwbchamber.com

Wythe County http://www.wytheco.org

Town of Wytheville http://www.wytheville.org

For more information contact the Graham Mansion at 276-284-0006 or

info@majorgrahammansion.com

Ghost Hunters!

In 2007, local paranormal investigations began performing formal investigations at the mansion. Over the course of three years, several paranormal groups have collected hundreds of EVPs (i.e., electronic voice phenomena), photographs, videos, and experienced paranormal contact at the mansion. The investigators believe they have communicated with the dominant spirits of Martha Peirce Graham, Squire David Graham, "Clara" a Civil War orphan befriended by Bettie and Emily Graham and secretly housed in their bedroom for several years, a slave boy and his mother, and various soldiers. In addition, the mansion staff have collected ghost stories and photos from the community and visitors and have anecdotal reports from guest clairvoyants. Is the mansion haunted? You can find out for yourself at the many ghost tours and investigations held each year at the Graham Mansion.

Good Times at the Graham Mansion

Above, "Tamara Azlin-Quinn" at SpookyWorld and below the many who make the Graham Mansion a scary place to visit each fall.

Josiah Cephas Weaver on the front porch of the Graham Mansion.

Josiah C. Weaver performing his Mountain Rock Music Show.

Mary Lin Brewer and Josiah Cephas Weaver.

Selected Bibliography

Manuscript Collections
    Graham Papers, University of Virginia
    Reid S. Fulton Papers, Virginia Tech
    Thomas D. Perry Papers, Virginia Tech

Private Collections
    Papers of Mary Lin Brewer and Josiah C. Weaver

Government
    1820 U. S. Census For Wythe County, Series M33 Roll
    #139
    U. S. Census Agricultural Schedules, 1860, 1870, 1880,
    1890

Newspapers and Magazines
    Big Blue Summer/Fall 2009
    Bristol Herald Courier: August 28, 2008;
    Christiansburg News Messenger: November 14, 2007;
    Des Moines, Iowa, Evening Tribune: July 13, 1921;
    Des Moines, Iowa, Register: August 30, 1921;
    Drake University Delphic: March 4, 1921;
    Newsweek: August 12, 1963;
    North Pinellas Times: July 30, 2006;
    Richmond Times Dispatch: July 16, 1978;
    Roanoke Times and World News: November 14, 1954;March 5,
    1978; October 28, 2007;
    Southwest Enterprise: January 13, 1974; March 14, 1978;
    August 13, 1981; January 4, 1997; July 4, 2006; August 30,
    2007;
    St. Petersburg (FL)Times: July 20, 2006;
    Sunday Times Journal: November 14, 1976;

Internet
    August Forsberg Diary
    http://miley.wlu.edu/forsberg/transcript.html
    Graham Genealogy
    freepages.genealogy.rootsweb.ancestry.com/~walker/graham
    www.sports.tambabay.com

Books and Papers

Fried, Sarah. *Constructing the Self: Female Identity Development in the Turn of the Century South*. Vanderbilt University, Nashville, 2002.
Ingles, Anne. *Journal of Bettie Ann Graham*. New York, 1978.
Kegley, Mary B.
  Early Adventures on the Western Waters, Volume III, Part 2. Wytheville, 2004.
  Glimpses of Wythe County, Virginia. Wytheville, 1986.
  Glimpses of Wythe County, Virginia, Volume Two. Wytheville, 1988.
  Wythe County, Virginia: A Bicentennial History. Wytheville, 1989.
Presgraves, James S. *Wythe County Chapters*. Wytheville, 1972.

Wythe County Historical Review
  No. 16, July 1979, pp 1-9
  No. 53, January 1998, pp. 11-18

Index

The mill at Graham's Forge

CPSIA information can be obtained at www.ICGtesting.com
Printed in the USA
LVOW062313150412

277729LV00008B/293/P